LOST OREGON TREASURE

ARTHUR H. REDMAN

Foreword by Julie A. Rhea

THE
History
PRESS

Published by The History Press
Charleston, SC
www.historypress.com

Copyright © 2024 by Arthur Redman
All rights reserved

Front cover: Oregon Historical Society No. 38194.
Back cover, top: Southern Oregon Historical Society #0043; *bottom*: *Grants Pass Courier*, 1904, 58962.

First published 2024

Manufactured in the United States

ISBN 9781467155519

Library of Congress Control Number: 2023945815

CONTENTS

FOREWORD

The allure of gold increased the pulse of prospectors, and they took pathways by the thousands to Oregon. It created a fever-inspired vision of mountains full of gold with nuggets as large as robin eggs nesting among the rock and gravel of streams and rivers. Pioneers, entire families, explorers, gamblers, storekeepers, teachers, ministers and women of ill repute loaded up their wagons and hit the trails, wetting their whistles and rolling along, all keeping in step on the pathways for gold.

The American explorer John C. Frémont created the pathways for gold and riches on his 1843 expedition in Northern California and Central Oregon. Decades later, the outsized headlines of the day's popular broadsheets, official newspapers and lurid tabloids broadcast new findings of gold, beckoning another wave of prospectors toward Central Oregon in search for the Lost Emigrant Mine or the Blue Bucket Placer.

Hundreds waited, wavering over their decision, until they could wait no longer. Countless people left with only the clothes on their back. Each seeker moved at the same pace as Frémont drove them forward. This newest expedition for gold by the bravest and the best was set in motion by the discovery of gold in California in 1848, five years before Frémont's third expedition.

Others, following the California forty-niners, traveled west in search for gold. They ended their current life and hopped on the trail of hope and fortune. They were pursuing legends of lost gold, not heading for previously located mines. Instead, they were sorting through stories and dead-end tales.

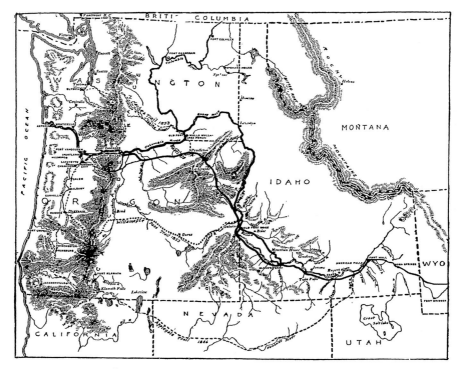

OREGON TRAIL ROUTES IN THE OREGON COUNTRY

Oregon Trail routes in Oregon. *Author's copy of* History of the Oregon Country *by Harvey Scott, 1924, opposite page 303.*

Finally, after great hardship and suffering—and not enough gold or money to continue—these people had no choice but to cease mining due to lack of money to maintain a living. They gathered the gold they had found and hauled it for safekeeping and returned to mining when economic conditions warranted rather than give up completely. Regrouping, they earned money by any means possible and, when ready, started over again. This cycle repeated itself until they died.

Finally, the original miners recognized that true and lasting treasure also existed above the ground. After spending so many years on a land they loved with people who had become devoted friends, they built homesteads, towns, churches and schools and prospered in the state of Oregon. If you find yourself marching along, whistling to the tune of the paths, stop by one of the mines or farms on your route and have a visit with a family that has lived nearby, many of whom have worked the land for over one hundred years.

Oregon Trail marker.
From History of the
Oregon Country, *1924, by*
Harvey Scott. Author's copy.

These farm owners receive a plaque that declares their property a "Century Farm." Gaze out over the vistas of mountains and valleys, horses, cattle and crops and let your eyes settle on the shining faces of the children, listen to the local radio station announcing where the next dance is, telling residents of lost dogs and letting people know who needs help rebuilding their barn lost to fire. Present-day treasures still exist in the West when one follows the paths and routes of John C. Frémont.

—Julie A. Rhea

Introduction

PATHWAYS TO LOST RICHES

John C. Frémont entered Central Oregon from California during the summer of 1843. His cartographer, Charles Preuss, was the first to show Mount McLoughlin on a map. Frémont named Summer Lake and Winter Ridge in Central Oregon. One year before, Frémont traveled east from The Dalles along the route of the future Oregon Trail.

The "Pathfinder's" steps were echoed by the journey of Stephen Meek and the wagon train Meek led in 1845. Somewhere along these routes is the probable location of the Lost Emigrant Mine, sometimes known as the Blue Bucket Placer, where members of the Meek Party found a gold nugget or two.

The quest for gold by the Wilson brothers began in San Francisco, California, which Frémont visited in 1842. The next path for gold before Oregon statehood in 1859 was the Lost Cabin Mine. This search led to the discovery of a scenic, sapphire-blue lake, christened Deep Blue Lake by prospector John Hillman in 1853. When rediscovered sixteen years later, it became Crater Lake. It became Oregon's first national park in 1903.

From a historic and, later, economic perspective, the hunt for gold was more important than the amount of gold found. Pedro de Castañeda, the chronicler of the Coronado expedition, wrote in 1542, "Granted they did not find the riches of which they have been told; rather, they found a place in which to search for them." East of the Oregon Cascade Mountains, these searches for gold and treasure had the upshot of discovering rich areas to explore and inhabit.

Mount Washington and lava beds in foreground. *By the author, 1962.*

The wealth in the Oregon Territory was the direct result of these early searches for mines. Gold discoveries on John Day River and in the Sumpter Valley were due to the ongoing search for the Blue Bucket Placer. Will Rogers said about gold, "There is a lot of difference in pioneering for gold and pioneering in spinach."

Settlement occurred at mining camps, which later became new towns like Jacksonville, John Day and Baker City and ghost towns like Auburn, whose population at one time exceeded ten thousand. The explorers saw treasures over and above gold, so they stayed and developed the land and their skills and sent for their families and friends, which led to the expansion of the state.

The following authentic stories and legendary quests are remarkable and expand on how Oregon became settled and on the significance of the character and bravery of the people who settled here. I learned about homesteader Elijah Bristow of Pleasant Hill, David Smith of Scio and the trailblazer Steve Meek. There is the lawyer turned renowned poet Samuel Simpson; the grizzled prospector Steve Oester; Ed Schieffelin, the founder of Tombstone, Arizona; and the sheepherder turned prospector Victor E. Casmyer. Additionally, there are the immigrant prospectors James "Bohemian" Johnson from Germany and two unnamed searchers known only as the Two Frenchmen. There are Native Americans who viewed it all. One, known as Indian John, Garguash, John Cash-Cash and Old Tenas Man became the centers of their own chronicles of lost mines.

Although "gold is where you find it," this is unquestionably useless advice to any seeker or student of lost mines. It is much more informative to observe that gold occurs only in areas where metamorphosed sedimentary, volcanic and intrusive rocks appear, forming granite rocks in and along fissures in the earth's crust.

These zones of broken rock caused by faulting, shearing and folding provide channels for the mineral-laden hot waters and vapors flowing upward from deep-lying igneous activity. Gold deposits result from associated mineralizing fluids exposed at the surface at the end of lengthy periods of uplift and erosion, because the intrusive rocks solidified at considerable depths.

In this narrative, all the reports of lost gold happen on the earth's surface, where a lucky prospector, cowboy or lost pioneer stumbled across a ledge, a cave of gold ore or a rich placer deposit. For these stories to have any factual basis according to geological science, lode deposits must occur in brittle, easily shattered rocks or in a pocket, which involves the action of circulating groundwater at or near the surface. In the case of placer deposits, running water usually carries the eroded material and much of the gold from its place of origin, leaving a vein behind if part of the original gold remains intact.

These lost mines, using modern geological knowledge, are evaluated by the author. These mine stories are factual, and the geological conditions support their existence. These include the Red Blanket and W.P. Paul's Mine. Mines such as the Four Dutchmen and the Mystery Mine of Bohemia Johnson are no longer lost, since their gold ore is now gone and the sites deserted.

The search for any lost mine can be made more accurate and vast lands areas eliminated when the areas of reported lost mines are coordinated with existing gold mining districts. Therefore, reported gold discoveries in the younger volcanic rocks of the high Cascades; gold around Crater Lake; or gold in the sandy soil of the Lost Forest are folklore to the eternal optimist placing a futile bet at the roulette wheel.

The story of gold includes social, emotional and economic factors deserving of consideration by students of history. Whether gold is present, lost or stolen, it becomes a legend of mystery, romance and adventure, appealing to inherent human needs to escape the tedium of everyday life and enter a world of hope and imagination. Riches awaiting discovery in the earth just beneath our feet or lying on the ground where even a child could fill water buckets with nuggets excite us all.

The human spirit detests failure. Hope and faith are universal among humanity. After the discovery of gold at Sutter's Mill in California, the search turned north to the Pacific Northwest. The second piece of gold found in Oregon was at Sailor Diggings or Waldo in the southern extreme of Josephine County, before the discovery by a member of Meek's wagon train became public.

These searchers followed pioneer trails, Native American trails, cow trails, deer trails—any trail. They dug where there were no trails, but frequently they sat and told stories to one another and, later, to journalists and writers about their lost gold hidden by landslides, silenced by a guide's death or lost due to the failure of memory from wandering in the heat of the desert without water or in the damp cold and snows of the forested wilderness.

These people are truly Frémont's pathfinders, for they trekked to search for wealth. If you are so bold as to feel at home by the fireplaces of Frémont's descendants, go ahead and follow the routes of the bold "Pathfinder." The first chapter about the allure of lost gold in Oregon begins several years after the California Gold Rush, in step with Frémont's trip to Eastern

Oregon to rediscover the first gold found in American territory, west of the Rocky Mountains, known as the Lost Emigrant Mine or Meek Cutoff Gold, in the late summer of 1845. The Lost Cabin Mine stories follow this. The book then discusses the Mystery Mine of Bohemia Johnson and the Red Blanket Mine and ends with personal advice about where to look for gold nuggets today.

1

LOST BLUE BUCKET MINE

The second gold discovery on the West Coast of the United States was the Blue Bucket Mine or placer deposit, found four years before the California Gold Rush of 1849 and after the gold discovery in 1842 at Placeritas Canyon just north of the Mexican pueblo of Los Angeles. The legend of the Blue Bucket Mine emerged after members of the Meek caravan spent time looking for gold while wandering around Eastern and Central Oregon searching for the wagon trail. They finally located the trail and arrived at The Dalles, Oregon, on October 7, 1845.

Stephen Hall Meek, a trapper, declared that he had firsthand knowledge of the Blue Mountains and insisted he had discovered a route that was at least two hundred miles shorter, and easier to pass through, than the track of the well-traveled Oregon Trail. It led across Eastern Oregon, and Meek would lead the wagons over his new trail. More than half of the members of a newly formed migrant wagon train decided to accept Stephen Meek's offer to serve as guide for the price of five dollars per wagon. His offer was irresistible, not only because of the shorter trail but also because he was the brother of famed trailblazer Joe Meek.

Meek organized the two hundred wagons into five trains and appointed a wagon expert for each train. The heads of these five trains were Solomon Tetherow and Colonel William G.T. Vault, with sixty-one wagons; Presley Welch, with twenty-five wagons; Samuel Hancock, with forty wagons; and Samuel Parker commanding forty-eight wagons.

Castle Rock, Malheur County. *Courtesy U.S. Department of Interior, Bureau of Land Management.*

Leading the two hundred wagons, Meek entered Oregon and proceeded up the Malheur River near Vale on August 24, 1845. They traveled twelve miles and camped the first night at Harper. From there, the caravan traveled up the Malheur River and headed northwest three miles up Hogg Creek to the South Fork of Cottonwood Creek. After traversing Castle Rock, crossing the Malheur River drainage into the Great Basin, Meek became lost. Beginning on September 7, the wagon train wandered west to the north side of Harney Lake from the mouth of Rattlesnake Creek, crossing alkali flats and the high desert to Wagontire Mountain. The trains then traveled northwest and eventually reached the Deschutes River, where they headed straight northward to the Columbia River at The Dalles.

Four years later, relatives returning from the California Gold Rush identified the yellow metal someone had picked up as gold. Newspaper articles appeared in print, and searches began. The first search was in 1851. Dan Herren, a member of the original party, led the second in 1854. In the 1860s, Native Americans drove the search parties back. The Adam-Griffin Party discovered gold on Canyon Creek, which led to Eastern Oregon's first gold rush. Some early searchers, including William F. Helm, trekked in 1863 to Canyon Creek, where they believed the true location of the Blue Bucket gold discovery existed.

Sketch of The Dalles Mission. *Oregon Historical Society.*

Stephen Meek returned to Eastern Oregon with a thirty-man expedition in 1868, and even though he led the wagon train, he failed to locate any gold. The most prevalent location mentioned in the maze of literature regarding the discovery, and where the area's earliest searches attempted to reach before being attacked by Native Americans, is west of the headwaters of the Malheur River.

Newspaper stories related to the Meek Party, who found and were present when the gold discovery occurred, are contradictory at best. Besides people's faulty memory, no one knew of any gold discoveries until at least four years later, and accounts are full of unintentional errors. One account states that the Meek Party used the gold as fish sinkers; another told of a thirteen-year-old girl who left her blue water bucket containing yellow stones by the stream and on her way back to camp picked up a large nugget. Her largest nugget became a doorstop in her Willamette Valley home after she married a Mr. Chapman. Her brother returned from the California gold fields sometime after 1850 and identified the stone as gold.

Mount Adams, Oregon.

Old postcard of Mount Adams, Washington, visible forty-five miles north of The Dalles, Oregon, as viewed by Oregon Trail migrants in 1845. *Author's collection.*

One memory that rings true is the account of Thomas Jefferson Fryer, who claims he saw the Blue Bucket gold. But he was only two years old at the time. Fryer heard accounts of the mine from his parents since childhood. He stated:

> *While near the head of the Malheur River the cattle wandered off one night. Daniel Herren, a cousin of W.J. Herren, went out to find the cattle. Just over the ridge from the head of the Malheur River, he came upon a little stream that ran toward the southwest. It did not empty into the Malheur. As he crossed the stream, he noticed something that looked like a yellow pebble in the stream. It was heavy and dull looking. Someone else picked up another nugget. [Hardin D.] Martin broke the nugget on a wagon wheel with a hatchet but instead of breaking it, it flattened out. He then threw it in a toolbox of the wagon.*

The family of William F. Helm, whose wagon traveled in the Tetherow train, had two water buckets painted blue, and this color became the central theme of the gold discovery, first appearing in the *Oregonian* as the Blue Bucket Mine in the letters column of April 12, 1885. These faulty and embellished accounts have complicated the search for the gold, creating

18

Stephen Meek, wagon train captain, in later years. *Oregon Historical Society*.

a legend. Samuel Hancock wrote a narrative of his experiences with the Tetherow train, and from his account and from the diaries of wagon master Samuel Parker and cattle driver Jessie Harritt, the general route could be determined with accuracy.

In 1906, Jonathan L. Riggs retold his grandfather's story about how the Blue Bucket got its name. Before Blue Bucket, the mine was the Lost Emigrant Mine, the Meek Cutoff Mine or simply the gold the Meek Party threw away. Riggs's grandfather, then fourteen, gave this account: "The train encamped on a small stream somewhere along the Harney Basin, there being hills to the northward and a level stretch of the desert to the south. A freshet had sluiced out the gulch, leaving the rock bare. A lady passing over this bare rock picked up pieces of yellow metal and came into camp carrying it in her apron and called attention to it." Asked how much she could pick up, "she pointed to a blue bucket saying she filled it up in a while."

No wonder the legend inspired so many searchers. The gold was so easy and plentiful that a child could pick it up by the bucketful. Samuel Parker wrote a letter signed "Blue Bucket" to the *Oregonian* newspaper published on May 6, 1885, responding to the Riggs letter.

The letter claims the wagon master, Mr. Parker, hammered the one-half-inch-square nugget flat on the iron rim of the wagon wheel after five or six young men found the nuggets in a small pool of water seven or eight miles northeast of the campsite and close to where a woman had died and was buried. There is no mention of the Herren family in Parker's story.

The significant factor in these accounts is the grave of Sarah King Chambers, the wife of Rowland Chambers. The grave was dug and marked by members of the Meek Party. Her gravestone, inscribed "Mrs. S. Chambers, September 3, 1845," is the only physical remnant left by the ill-fated wagon train, and its location was not known until 1950. According to many stories, the Blue Bucket Mine is west one or two days' travel by covered wagon from this grave. Sarah Chambers's grave is near the North Fork of the Malheur, one mile north of the community of Beulah. Seekers have searched west from Chambers's grave. In the 1880s, H.B. Reeves, a prosperous Malheur County rancher, traced the exact route of the ill-fated wagon train to the grave of Sarah Chambers. Although Reeves prospected to the west, he failed to find any gold.

One of the more recent searches was the Scientific Safari of 1958. The safari included William Lambert, an electronics specialist; Lancaster Pollard, a Northwest historian; P.A. Buckmaster, a prospector; Walter Eastman, a mining investor; Steve Roth, a photographer; and two hunters and prospectors familiar with the area. In 1957, after three weeks tracing wagon ruts to Sarah Chambers's grave, the safari members studied the diaries of the Meek Party as well as maps, letters and newspaper articles and coordinated with modern geological knowledge to determine where the wagon train may have passed over gold-bearing rock.

The safari decided to set up camp west of Chambers's grave on Otis Creek, ten miles north of Drewsey by way of a rutted ranch trail. They used M-scopes, microscopes, metal detectors, mortar and pestle, gold pans, picks and shovels to prospect, pulverizing sample rocks to dust and washing them in gold pans. Buckmaster even smelled the rock to determine if the chemical odor was the same as that of gold-bearing rock.

Mrs. Chambers's grave, the *Oregonian*, October 5, 1950, page 13. The only marked grave of the ill-fated Meek wagon train of 1845, identified by descendants in 1950. *Photo from* Terrible Trail *by Kenneth Clark and Lowell Tiller, 1966, author's copy.*

In one week, they prospected a 325-square-mile area, which included the North Fork as far north as Lost Creek, the main branch of the Malheur River and all named tributaries and unnamed tributaries: Blue Bucket, Griffin, Otis, Birch, Cottonwood, Tamarack, Calamity, Squaw and Spring Creeks. The eight-man safari found colors but nothing comparable to the gold nuggets found by members of the Meek Party. No creek even yielded enough to make panning profitable. The safari eliminated the area immediately north and west of Sarah Chambers's grave as the site of the Blue Bucket Mine. Lancaster Pollard wrote: "The lost Blue Bucket Mine was not on any of the creeks within the area covered. Historical research and scientific prospecting have failed. The lost Blue Bucket is somewhere else."

Charlie Shepherd gave up the search for the Blue Bucket gold in 1960. The eighty-three-year-old prospector heard about the mine from a man who got off the stage in 1901 at Bully Creek. This man said he found gold there while a member of Meek's wagon train as a child and spent one summer looking for gold before giving up. Shepherd also searched Bully Creek and later Dixie Creek in Rye Valley. He found gold near his longtime home near Hailey, Idaho. But, like others, he found no gold in Malheur County east or west of Chambers's grave.

THE SOUTH FORK?

Ruby El Hult, author of *Lost Mines and Buried Treasures of the Pacific Northwest*, suggests that the Blue Bucket Mine lies south of Sarah Chambers's grave. But the area south of Beulah is not gold-bearing terrain. The Eagle-Picher Diatomite Mine is located just ten miles southwest of Beulah. Keith Clark and Lowell Tiller traced the entire route in 1966 and concluded that the Meek Party did not travel south from Chambers's grave, as that terrain was impassable for wagons. Clark and Tiller maintained that the Meek Party went northward, up the North Fork of the Malheur River, then five miles north around the southern shoulder of Castle Rock, then southeast to Cottonwood Creek, an east branch of the Middle Fork of the Malheur. The group then traveled southwest into Drewsey Valley, continuing west of the town of Drewsey and over the hill to upper Pine Creek south by way of either East Cow Creek or Big Rock Creek into the Harney Basin. These are the conclusions of Clark and Tiller in their book *Terrible Trail* and in a later book published by the Webb Research Group in 1992.

There has always been confusion about which fork of the Malheur the Meek caravan followed. For example, Jessie Harritt mentions in his diary entry of September 3, "Travel seven miles and encamped on the South Fork of Malheur." The middle fork of the Malheur flows north to Juntura; it was labeled as the South Fork on army maps until 1860. The error lies with the publication of *Lt. Joseph Dixon Survey Map of 1860*, which also printed the same mistake that Dixon originally made in 1859, mistaking the South Fork of the Malheur River for the Middle Fork.

Meek referred to an obsolete army map that was inaccurate in critical details; he believed he was on the South Fork. The army map showed the South Fork flowing out of Malheur Lake, and Meek pointed out this belief to members of the search party. Both Jessie Harritt and James F. Fields overheard this claim; both were members of the Riggs train. Fields wrote in his journal on September 4, "Camped upon the head of a small branch of the South Fork of the Malheur." On later maps, the North Fork is a branch of the South Fork. Furthermore, the newer maps also show the location of Sarah Chambers's gravesite.

This mention of the South Fork has led searchers to look for the mine southward all the way to Steens Mountain. Captain O.C. Applegate, a pioneer historian from Klamath Falls, wrote in the *Oregonian* of May 16, 1919, that he leaned toward the belief that the discovery was around Steens Mountain. F.H. Latham wrote in *True Treasure* magazine in 1966 that the Meek trains left Agency Valley traveling up Warm Springs Creek along the Malheur River branch divide between the Main Fork and South Fork looking for water. The gold discovery occurred somewhere southward to the headwaters of Coleman Creek on the night of September 3. The next day, the party reached Coyote or Crane Creek and reached Crane Prairie on the fifth, if one believes the South Fork theory and the diaries of Fields and Harritt.

A latter-day searcher, L.L. Mills, in 1958 looked northeast from Steens Mountains all the way to the Maury Mountains in the Ochoco National Forest, where he came across a gold mine operated by a miner from Bend. Mills believed this was the real site of the Blue Bucket Mine, despite the fact that the Meek gold is a placer deposit near water and not a lode mine located high in the mountains. The gold discovery occurred later in the trek, when everyone was looking for water beginning at Wagontire Mountain north to a location between the South Fork of the Crooked River and the Deschutes River.

The Discoverers

The important factors in the quest for the Blue Bucket Mine are who was present or who discovered the gold. The *Oregonian* published Dan Herren's obituary, "Found Blue Bucket Mine," on July 21, 1908. It credits Dan Herren, age twenty-one, who came west with his uncle John Herren, for discovering the gold. John Herren later stated that his nephew found the gold in muddy cattle tracks and showed them around camp. Other members of the wagon train may have brought an additional specimen or two back to the wagon of Hardin D. Martin.

The first printed account of the Blue Bucket Mine appeared in the *Portland Bee* on February 6, 1869. The reporter, D.S. Clark, wrote that Daniel Herren "was looking for lost cattle while the company was camped here [at the head of the Malheur River, and], picked up a piece of shining metal on the rocky bed of a creek. He carried to camp as a curiosity." The *Bee* article is the most accurate of the written accounts, except for its location of the gold. Clark wrote, "The discovery occurred 'near the head of the Malheur River, an error which caused much trouble and disappointment among prospectors' over the years."

A statement published by a granddaughter of John Herren Flora Bailey, stated that Dan Herren saw a piece of metal shining in a mound pushed up by a mole or gopher and that all the stories start with just one oblong nugget about the size of a man's thumb noticed on top of a mole hill. In theory, tracing the route of the Herren family should lead to gold. The task became impossible, even for Dan and Benjamin Herren, who returned to Eastern Oregon leading a party of prospectors in 1854. The brothers failed to find any gold nuggets, because Native Americans stole their horses at Dry Summit, east of Burns, forcing them to travel by foot back to Portland.

Flora E. Bailey described the area: "There was a group of small stone houses on a bench above the stream, sheltered by a still higher bank and by trees." Her father, Levi, then ten years old, is the only person who remembers the stone huts. They were round, having a diameter of six to seven feet and covered over the top. They were on the headwaters of the Malheur River or one of the smaller streams that form it.

No one has given an account of these unusual little huts during the search for the Blue Bucket gold except for Summer Houston of Prineville, who told his brother Ben, of Bend, Oregon, that he discovered a group of stone huts on upper Silver Creek, and inside one of them was a newspaper clipping about Dan Herren. No archaeological information on these alleged huts exists. A member of the Herren family found the gold two or three miles east of Buck Creek on a tributary of Silver Creek while looking for water after the wagon trains split at GI Ranch. If the stone huts existed at that time, it is possible that the upper bench may have slipped into the creek or was buried in a landslide—or the huts are only a geological formation.

Ruth Herren, the daughter of John Herren, wrote a letter to the *Oregonian*, published on April 28, 1919, that John's nephew Dan found the gold. "It was somewhere in the Tygh Valley." The gold "was found in some tracks made by the cattle in going to water." The metal was of no interest at the time, because no one knew the value of the pieces and because the people were tired and worn out with winter coming and their provisions running out. There is no mention of a search for water or a creek, because there is adequate water in the Deschutes River, contradicting the account of Dan Herren's search of 1854 and of subsequent searches. The Meek Party camped at Oak Springs Creek northeast of Maupin on October 4 and eliminated Tygh Valley near the end of the trek as the site of the gold discovery.

Other members of the Herren family had their gold discovery stories. W.H. Herren, in a letter to the *Oregonian* on March 7, 1922, stated that his father, twenty-three-year-old W.J. Herren, and W.J.'s sister Susan, who later married William Wallace, went out to hunt for water two miles in a northerly direction. "They finally found a dry creek bed which they followed until they found a place where a little water was seeping through the gravel, and while my father was digging for water, his sister saw something bright and picked it up."

The siblings returned to camp with two nuggets. They showed them to the older men, who told them that if the nuggets were gold, they would be malleable. One of the men took a hammer and flattened both nuggets into saucer-shaped discs. The discovery of water closer than two miles north of a camp meant that no one returned to the site. W.H. Herren and his sister are the only members of the party who ever saw the exact spot where the nuggets existed, according to this account.

The Helm family claimed that their children were looking for water while Mrs. W.F. Helm was washing clothes when one of the girls picked up gold nuggets and placed them in a blue water bucket. William F. Helm and his son Benjamin also claimed to have found gold on the Immigrant Creek side of the ridge of mountains toward Silver Creek. One grizzled prospector, "Old Man Pierce," reviewed the Helm family accounts and sought the gold instead on Summit Prairie near a location known locally as Prospect Meadows.

In 1890, a prospector known only as Mr. White started a gold rush when he claimed the Blue Bucket Placer was upstream on Rattlesnake Creek. Peter Mortimer also arrived to prospect on the first ravine east of Rattlesnake Creek. Neither man found any gold. White disappeared, and Mortimer stayed behind to live in a sod house on the east side of the creek named for him. Fort Harney, built on Rattlesnake Creek in 1867 and occupied by soldiers until 1880, proves there is no gold in the immediate vicinity.

In contrast, Big Rock Creek, Little Rock Creek and East Cow Creek appear neglected by prospectors. George Irwin of Monument said in an article in the *Oregonian* dated April 23, 1919, that the discovery in Spanish Gulch is the site of the true location of the Blue Bucket Mine. Placer gold found at Spanish Gulch five miles southeast of Antone at Rock and Birch Creeks dates from the 1860s. W.W. Oglesby of Cottage Grove placed the discovery in the watershed of the John Day River.

One searcher, Charles W. Brown of Canyon City, talked to Benjamin Helm, who as a teenager in the Meek caravan believed the Blue Bucket site was on either Canyon Creek or Spanish Gulch. Unfortunately, Brown and others were looking at the correct landmarks where gold exists near Camp Creek but in the wrong location, twenty or more miles northeast of the actual site.

One other camp story, set along the banks of a tributary of John Day River, is by George H. Himes, and it discredits the whole area as the location of gold. Himes writes: "Numerous yellow pebbles were found along the creek's edge and among the grass roots. An attempt to catch some fish failed because the current was very swift, and the effort failed." Then W.G. T'Vault, Thomas R. Cornelius and James Terwilliger, a blacksmith, conceived the idea of using one of the bright pebbles as fishing sinkers and, finding it soft, pounded it thin and used it as a sinker on fishing lines. This account is at best a whopper of a fish story. There is no mention of attempting to fish in any of the written diaries, even if the three men had the time and desire to do so.

Eighteen-year-old Hugh McNary also told of a member of the Herren family finding gold. James Terwilliger, because he was a blacksmith with one of the companies, is the person who, according to Lawrence McNary, hammered the gold on the iron rim of a wagon wheel to examine the metal near a tributary of the John Day River.

The Meek caravan camped at Malheur Lake on September 7 at Wright Point. The next day's travel, according to Harritt, advanced ten miles west, where we "encamped on a small stream affording good grass and a few small willows." The next day, the party went on to a small spring six miles west. Lawrence McNary places the site of the wagon train separation at a locality called Stinking Hollows. This location was found by the Silvies River three days after September 10. The mileage given by Jessie Harritt does allow time for a westward trek to Wagontire Mountain, which is correct only if Stinking Hollows is located on one of the sloughs of the Silvies River instead of on the western side of Little Silver Lake. As soon as the migrants finished setting up camp, the worn-out oxen teams laid down and refused to get up, delaying the wagon trains.

McNary concedes that individual companies under separate command may have traveled due west as far as the Wagontire region, but according to Harritt's diary, they were all together. Harritt noted on September 10 that while all the trains were together they made a "west course over a tolerable level road" for twenty-five miles that was very stony in places. They found no grass or water, contrary to McNary's northwest-bound thesis from the lower Silvies River valley. The water at Crane Spring on the western shore of dry Silver Lake was their last source for twenty-five miles. The campsite was at a small, clear spring surrounded by a little grass. Several willows stood on the western side of a dry alkaline lakebed, six miles northwest of the Double O Station, where the water bubbles out of the earth and flows about fifty feet, then sinks in the desert. This is the right spot and description of Stinking Hollows, where there was not enough water for one thousand men, women, children, 3,100 head of cattle, oxen and 1,000 goats, forcing the wagons trains to move west in their desperate search for water.

Other searchers, beginning with the 1860 expedition led by Henry Marlin, started on the northeastern side of Wagontire Mountain. They found discarded wagon tires left by the McNary Party, providing the name to the mountain. In the spring of 1861, a party of forty-five men led by A.A. Smith, including Eugene Skinner and Joseph D. Myers, found six deserted wagons from a wagon train. The wagons were about four years old at the time, dating them to about 1857 and so not from the Meek train.

The A.A. Smith expedition traveled east to Silver Creek, where Zachariah Moreland, a member of the Meek Party who became a prospector, claimed to have seen a creek full of gold that ran almost due north one half day's travel from a rocky butte then known as Chicken Hawk Butte. Near the butte, Moreland and Skinner found near one stream square bits of yellow rock that proved to be only iron pyrite ("fool's gold").

Wagontire Mountain looking west from US 395, elevation 6,504 feet. *Oregon Department of Transportation.*

So much for Moreland's accurate memory of a creek of gold in the Silver Creek drainage. The party moved north, prospecting unsuccessfully at Crooked River and Burnt River.

Samuel Hancock of the Tetherow Party writes about the Wagontire Mountain area: "Journeying along in a most wretched way imaginable both ourselves and stock destitute of water, we were about to despair when we came to small springs, where we encamped, though there was little grass; but we had water, and it was hard to leave it." The largest spring is Foster Spring on the north side of Wagontire Mountain at Lost Creek Spring known as "Sinking Hollows" or "Lost Hollows," twenty miles to the northwest, which the wagons reached on September 12, 1845.

The latter-day quest for the Blue Bucket Mine follows "the search for water," since the area west of the Malheur River has never yielded gold in sufficient quantities to pinpoint the location of the gold nugget found by Dan Herren or those found by anyone else. Lawrence McNary, reviewing the diary of his father, Hugh M. McNary, recalled the hammering of the gold on the iron rim of the wagon wheel after reading Jessie Harritt's diary. The date of this important occurrence was the morning or night of September 17, 1845. Jessie Harritt and the McNary family camped at the northeast side of Wagontire Mountain on September 15 at the headwaters of Foster Spring and one day later at Lost Creek, according to Harritt's diary, after traveling twenty-five miles west from Crane Spring at the now dry Silver Lake in Harney County. They camped at Silver Lake for six days before dusk on September 9, 1845, in a small grove of willows.

Job McNamee of the T'Vault-led train returned to Stinking Hollows, an area of alkali springs, after searching with other men for water. They saw "three wagons had been placed facing each other in the form of a triangle, their tongues raised and tied together at the top."

The angry men of the party had put a rope around Meek's neck to lynch him by hanging. McNamee pointed his rifle at the men and halted the execution and said: "Meek is the only man who has ever been in this part of the country before. If you hang him, we are all dead men. If you give him a little time, he may be able to recognize some landmark here and find a way out."

The men gave Meek three additional days. Harritt wrote on September 14 that men accompanied Meek, "the pilot in search of water but found none, they returned late in the evening." Samuel Hancock hid Meek and his wife after September 15 to prevent another hanging attempt that morning, which saved Meek's life.

Meek was lost and just guessing by heading north of Wagontire Mountain in the quest to find water. Meek and his wife reappeared when the Hancock wagon was emptying for caulking at this crossing of the Deschutes River at Maupin on October 3.

George Millican, who settled in Eastern Oregon in 1868, talked to Billy Vaughan and Sol Tetherow, who both saw the Blue Bucket gold. They stated that when the gold was found, Meek was with the wagon train, although in hiding, at the time the gold was found. The gold discovery occurred before the train camped at the South Fork of the Crooked River. Millican's younger brother Robert, a member of the Solomon Tetherow train with the Helm family, was with the 1860 party led by Henry Marlin to search for the gold.

This sixty-man expedition, including 160 horses and mules, began at Eugene and backtracked over the Meek Cutoff from the Deschutes River to the Silvies River. William Vaughn thought that the Hampton area had the right, familiar look, but he was not certain of the exact spot where the gold arrived. He decided to look with Henry Marlin eastward beyond the point where the various trains separated in looking for water at The Sinks of Lost Creek. North of Malheur Lake at Rattlesnake Creek, Native Americans stampeded all but twenty of their horses and forced the men to head back to Eugene City on foot, becoming one of the parties failing to find gold in Eastern Oregon west of the Malheur River.

The wagons, according to McNary, traveled thirty miles northwest along the Silvies River and then to Silver Creek, then north to reach the headwaters of the Crooked River on the morning of September 17. There the gold discovery occurred. His interpretation of the Harritt diary places the area of search at a western tributary of the eighty-four-mile-long Silver Creek in the Silver Creek volcanic vicinity.

Prospecting on Sage Hen Creek occurred in 1916 for nitrates, five miles north of Riley. The nitrates occur in streaks and pockets in the gray volcanic ash among lava fragments that, once partly melted, proved there was no gold in this volcanic area near lower Silver Creek.

THE GREAT SEPARATION

The Meek Party mixed up names of prominent landmarks. They knew Castle Rock as Frémont Peak and Steens Mountain as the Snowy Mountains, believed at the time to be part of the Cascade Range. The South Fork of

Oregonian, July 21, 1908.
Page 10

Found Blue Bucket Mine
Death of Dan Herrin Recalls Early Day Stampedes For Gold

Dan Herrin Who died at his farm home, near Tonquin Washington County, July 10, was one of Oregon's oldest pioneers, and had resided on his farm continuously for more than forty years.

He was born in Decatur County Ind December 7, 1924. When a young man he went to Missouri, and from there came with his family of his uncle, John Herren, across the plains to Oregon in 1845.

He went to the Cayuse War in 1847 and, was one of the escorts which accompanied to Oregon City for burial the remains of Colonel Gillham, killed from the accidental discharge of his own gun.

It was during the journey from Missouri to Oregon in 1845, when the emigrant train had lost its' way and was wandering among the headwaters of the Malheur River, that Dan Herren picked up pieces of yellow metal that afterward gave rise to all the golden stories of the "Blue Bucket Mines." He himself later searched for the spot, and hundreds of others have devoted years to the quest, but the location has never been discovered.

Mr. Herren found mining for several years, living mostly on the frontier. Then returning to the Willamette Valley, he was married to Miss Westfall and among the Tualatin Hills.

Six children were born to them, five of whom are still living. One daughter, Mrs. Sealy, and her husband having died before. Mr. Herren's varied experiences in the pioneer days of Oregon made him an interesting companion, and he retained his facilities in an unusual degree, until seized by last illness which was of short duration.

He was buried July 12, 1908. A large attendance of relatives, friends and neighbors being present.

the Malheur River is confused with its Middle and North Forks and the Silvies River with the Crooked River, while the South Fork of the Crooked River was the Sandy. Likewise, members of the northbound Meek caravan for years confused the main Crooked River as a tributary of the John Day River when they reached the mouth of Camp Creek, traveling down the Crooked River to Post, trekking north to Ochoco Creek and then west five miles to Prineville. The Harritt Party headed north from Wagontire

Mountain on the night of September 16, thereby passing Glass Butte on the east to Hampton Buttes and crossing Buck Creek. They camped at the current GI Ranch, where the wagon trains separated.

The McNary, Riggs, Harritt and Parker Parties continued north the next day to the South Fork of the Crooked River, known to them as the Sandy River. This train, according to the diary of Jessie Harritt, a young cattle driver, traveled north from Wagontire Mountain on September 16, arriving at Buck Creek on the morning of the seventeenth, reaching the Crooked River by evening.

Harritt wrote on September 17, "We yoked our teams at two o'clock, traveled six miles and encamped on the Sandy [Crooked River], a delightful stream running to the northwest, affording an abundance of fine grass but no wood."

The last camp where all the wagon trains were together was on Buck Creek, near the present site of the large GI Ranch. The trains then reunited at Sagebrush Springs south of Madras. From GI Ranch, a group of forty wagons led by Samuel Hancock and sixty-six wagons of the Solomon Tetherow train headed westward toward the northeast side of Hampton Butte, then west to where Ant Creek meets Bear Creek, traveling west along Bear Creek.

Near Alfalfa, sixteen miles east of Bend, someone from the Tetherow and Hancock trains carved in a juniper tree limb, "Lost Meeks 1845." This marker is on the westbound route toward Pilot Butte, where Warm Springs Indians told members of the wagon train they would find water there. A Native American who spoke a little English told them that if they went with him to a high ridge, nearby they could see down into the Deschutes and Crooked River valleys.

The Native American showed them buttes that lay south of Prineville and said they could find water there but no water between there and the Deschutes. He also showed them Pilot Butte and told them that if they would head straight for that butte, they would find water and a place to cross. Tetherow wrote in 1847, "So far from refusing to follow the advice of the Indian, at my request, he was employed by Mr. Meek to pilot us to Crooked River, which he did for a blanket." This proves that Meek was with the Tetherow and Hancock wagons at this point.

Also in this train were members of the Herren family, including Dan, who found a gold nugget or two. Whether this southern separation is near the location of the Blue Bucket discovery by Dan Herren, and whether Meek was present at the gold discovery site, is open to debate.

The Herren family, along with the Tetherow and Hancock trains, crossed the Deschutes River at the present-day town of Bend and traveled north down the Deschutes to rejoin the main caravan. Jessie Harritt wrote on September 26 that the party was camping at "a good spring in company with about 200 wagons."

His account proves that all the wagons were together at that date and arrived at The Dalles together, disapproving a theory by Bert Weber, Lois Pierce and Earl Stanley Gardner that a party including the Hamilton and Riggs families and Dr. McBride headed south from Wagontire Mountain onward to Goose Lake and Yreka, California.

Ada Bradley Millican told the *Oregonian* in 1919 that Straub Price, who had a ranch at Hampton Butte, said that one party of prospectors found an ox yoke near Hampton Buttes that had Solomon Tetherow's name carved on it. Price also told Millican that a landslide had occurred on one of the buttes and that this may have covered up the gold discovery site. The area from Hampton Buttes north to the Crooked River has been the site of two gold discoveries.

George Millican dug a nugget from a boulder above a spring at Hampton Buttes. If Millican found one nugget, there must have been more in the Hampton Buttes area, and the presence of water is consistent with all accounts of the Blue Bucket legend. It is unknown why Millican, who had been a miner in his youth in California and elsewhere, did not follow up and engage in mining activity before he sold his ranch in 1916 after finding gold.

In addition, Mrs. Cecil McKenzie found tiny gold nuggets in chicken droppings at her family's homestead near the mouth of Camp Creek, where the Meek Party had found water. In 1858, Andrew McClure and Jason Peters, who was with the Meek caravan, prospected from Prineville across Combs Flat and up the Crooked River to Camp Creek, crossing the east side of Maury Mountain back east to the Camp Creek Valley and south to the South Fork of the Crooked River.

McClure and company found nothing but a little color in their gold pans. Today, the Hampton Butte area is a popular rockhound site for jasper and green petrified wood but not gold. But George Millican found or claimed to have found gold among these eroded hills.

The placer lies to the north of the 6,333-foot-high Hampton Butte at an area south of Camp Creek below the lavas. Hampton Buttes is of volcanic origin and is not part of gold-bearing terrain, rising 2,300 feet above the High Lava Plains north of Millican. The farther northeast one searches, the more likely gold deposits are to occur.

A prospector named Howard discovered gold twenty-six miles east of Prineville in 1872. These placers are in the forested hills centering on Ochoco Creek and upstream on Scissors Creek, which crosses the mineralized area of tertiary andesitic fracture zones altered by carbonate-quartz-sulfide veins and enters Ochoco Creek from the southwest to the old mining camp of Scissorsville. In addition, the Ophir-Mayflower lode mine, located on the west bank of Ochoco Creek and within the Howard District, produced twenty thousand ounces of lode gold before 1923, being the only location twenty miles west of the Meek Party path where commercial gold mining has occurred. Gold nuggets exist on a southern tributary of Ochoco Creek west of the north-flowing Scissors Creek and may be near the site of the Blue Bucket discovery. The wagons of the north Meek Party crossed Ochoco Creek about five miles east of present-day Prineville at Combs Flat.

The Ochoco Mountains is also where the "Four Dutchmen" discovered gold. The quartet left the California gold fields after the rush in search of more gold. They spent the summer digging a fortune out of a canyon. During the late fall season and with the approach of harsh weather, as well as a lack of food, they decided to return to California. They hid their tools, shovels and gold pans under a log, intending to return. But sickness and death broke up the foursome, and they never made it back.

ANOTHER BLUE BUCKET SAGA

Lois Allen Pierce of Hoodsport, Washington, had family journals in her possession indicating a different route of Stephen Meek's guided wagon trains across Southeastern Oregon. The route, known as the Meek Cutoff, is where members found gold somewhere in Eastern Oregon. Pierce was descended from James Miller Allen and Hannah Jane Riggs. Allen, her paternal grandparents and members of the Riggs family were headed by James Berry Riggs. Young Lois Allen believed these stories after hearing them firsthand from her uncles Milton Riggs and Cyrus Albert Allen. They and other pioneer relatives found a group of forty-three wagons guided by Meek on September 3, 1845, two days ahead of the main train heading south of Malheur Lake at Crane Prairie on a southwest trek across the Donner und Blitzen River headed to Warner Lakes, 120 miles to the south.

Her assertions do not fit the historical record, especially the account of James F. Field, a member of the Riggs train. Field wrote on September 16, 1845, mentioning Captain Riggs. Field's mileage accounts agree with other diary writers, indicating that the separation of the wagon train did not occur on September 3, 1845. The Lois Pierce book *Lost Immigrants of 1845 and the Blue Bucket of Gold* is a dubious account of the Blue Bucket epic. In addition, the diary of Jessie Harritt mentions Meek on September 14, 1845, ten days after the Pierce family accounts date their southwest departure from the main wagon train.

On September 26, 1845, all two hundred wagons of the Meek caravan camped at Sagebrush Springs, north of Madras. The diary of Jessie Harritt mentions Meek on September 14, 1845, ten days after the Pierce family accounts date their southwest departure from the main wagon train. Meek could not have been part of this party, since he was in the other group.

The gold discovery, according to Lois Pierce, occurred when Rufus Riggs dug a large water hole among the black rocks of the sands of a streambed in a canyon meandering in a north–south direction. Later, while camping near the water source, young Hannah Allen brought six shining rocks back to camp from the water hole. They were later identified as gold.

Lois Pierce's later research, financed by the mystery writer Erle Stanley Gardner and *Desert Magazine*, led to an area where gold exists in Lake County between Rabbit and Foley Hills. According to Allen and Riggs family writings, a woman, man and child of the southbound wagon train died on consecutive days before the discovery of water on the northern slopes of Wagontire Mountain at the sinkholes of Lost Creek.

Working backward, E.S. Gardner assumed the train traveled twelve miles a day, which would put the three graves about twelve miles apart. The second Pierce-led party found a grave near a windmill on an old ranch south of Christmas Valley. Twelve miles farther south, a second grave was located near the Alkali Lake station, and another twelve miles south the third grave exists off US Highway 395. In 1958, L.L. Mills found an unidentified grave two days' travel east, leading him to discover an operating gold mine in the Maury Mountains sixty miles to the north, which proves only that pioneer graves exist throughout Eastern and Central Oregon if one looks long enough.

The area between Foley Creek and Rabbit Creek is covered with potholed lava beds. The area is about ten miles north of Plush. The Loftus brothers found gold in this area in 1906, starting a small mining rush. There are no production records for the Coyote Hill or Lost Cabin District. Rocks in the district include tuffs and breccias, and the area has rhyolitic flows and small intrusive activity of the tertiary age with rocks cut by small, disjoined fractures filled with clay limonite and quartz. The small amount of gold recovered has not been in placer deposits near water, as recounted in all Blue Bucket narratives, but in clay seams along with copper oxide minerals.

Two other married couples besides D.H. and Lois Pierce staked claims and called themselves the Blue Bucket Group after finding colors in a gold pan and finding one piece of gold about the size of a match head on the Hogback Road north of Plush. The area, containing the only group of juniper trees for miles around, a stream running south, black rocks and sand in the creek bed, was one day's travel west from a camp made in a swampy area identified by Ms. Pierce as Blue Joint Lake. Erle Gardner found no gold in the lava potholes.

He believed that Foley Creek Canyon was the source of the lost wagon train gold, while writer Choral Pepper of *Desert Magazine* held out for Rabbit Creek, the next creek to the north. One reviewer of Lois Pierce's family diary asked, "With the horrendous number of and magnitude of errors in this Oregon story, how dependable can the other tales be?"

The tracks and graves south of Wagontire Mountain may have resulted from members of a small group of wagons of the Meek-led party who decided before September 15, 1845, to abandon the rest of the party and head south to California. But Lois Pierce wrote that the Allen family arrived at The Dalles on November 8, one month later than the other wagon trains. Jessie Harritt, in his diary of the trek of the Meek Caravan, wrote on September 26, while on the Deschutes River, that "they encamped at a good spring in company with about 200 wagons," proving that all the wagons were together at this point and date.

One writer for *Lost Treasure* magazine recounted in 1988 that Solomon Tetherow led sixty-six wagons south to a spring at little Silver Lake in Harney County on September 11, 1845, and traveled via Horse Head Mountain to Juniper Mountain in adjoining Lake County, because in the diaries there is a mention of stunted juniper trees. Days before this southbound trek, according to writer Mike Ratzlaff, Dan Herren and his sister found gold in a rocky streambed twenty or more miles to the south or near alkali lakes while looking for drinking water.

The problem with Ratzlaff's thesis is that the stunted juniper trees that gave their name to a mountain are located in Western Oregon, and therefore do not apply to Juniper Mountain in Lake County. Three members of the Meek train described to the *Oregon Spectator* the landscape south of Silver Lake in 1847 as "an immense scope of level or gently undulating country, as far as the vision of the eye could extend." It would make more sense for the immigrants to head west following the leading wagons of the caravan

Mount Washington, which served as a landmark for the Lost Emigrant wagon train of 1845. *Photo by author.*

to Wagontire Mountain, where there was water, then to head south into the dry unknown.

The Tetherow-led train arrived at Wagontire Mountain one day later to rejoin the rest of the caravan at the GI Ranch. The southbound wagon tracks from Wagontire Mountain and the three graves found by Erle Stanley Gardner and the Pierces were from another wagon train than the Meek-led party, heading south to California sometime later.

James Field ceased to make diary entries after September 24, 1845, when he became ill. Field's diary to this date agrees with Samuel Parker and Jessie Harritt concerning miles traveled and landmarks observed and allows for no southward travel from Wagontire Mountain by the Meek Party. The California-bound wagon train and the persons in the three unknown graves were not members of the Allen or Riggs families and are an additional mystery of the Blue Bucket Mine saga.

THE BLUE BUCKET MINE IN NEVADA?

In June 1864, Dr. R.H. Burney, dentist Henry Dain (or Dane) and twelve partners traveled over eight hundred miles prospecting for the Blue Bucket

Mine from Canyon City, Crooked River and as far south as the Black Rock Desert in Nevada. Burney stated that it might surprise some "to learn their 'Lost Camp' was as far south as California, and the timbered ridge they crossed was the Sierra Nevada." Due to Indian attacks, Burney and his party decided to return north to Oregon to prospect along the North Fork of the Malheur River, where most migrants of the Meek-led wagon train believed the gold nuggets existed.

The two-hundred-member wagon train led by Stephen Meek crossed Eastern Oregon during late August and September 1845. Writers including Harry Drago, Erle Stanley Gardner and Bert Webber confuse members of the Meek Party with those of another wagon train party led by Captain Elisha Sowers across Nevada. Members of the Meek Party, in this scenario, ended up in Yreka, according to writers Robert W. and Adam Smith Hamilton and Dr. James McBride.

The Sowers-led wagon train kept together on the California Trail until reaching the future site of Winnemucca, Nevada, where they split from the main group heading south down the Humboldt River to Sacramento in early October 1845. The contingent, bound for Northern California and Southern Oregon, turned northwest into the Black Rock Desert, pioneering a route across the Black Rock Mountains near High Rock Canyon. Here three children found enough gold to fill the bottom of their water bucket. This party's route closely followed sections of the Applegate and Lassen Trails to Southern Oregon and Northern California, first used in 1846.

On their fourth day in the Black Rock Desert, this party, which split off from the other group, reached a canyon so deep and narrow that their oxen team had to be unhitched and doubled up to get one wagon through at a time. The children of the train, having little notion of Paiute Indian attacks, climbed out of their wagons and, following behind, out of the way, began picking up yellow pebbles and tossed them into the blue water buckets that dangled at the sides of the wagons, thus discovering the Blue Bucket Mine of Nevada. The wagon wheel rims left shiny tire marks and golden streaks in spots, which meant nothing to the pioneers. Across open sage land, they continued to the northwest, entering California at present-day Eagleville and westward to Yreka, where they spent the winter on the Klamath River.

Dr. Henry Dain (or Dane), a dentist in Yreka, made a visit to a member of the Sowers-led party. The children had saved the pebbles they had tossed into the water buckets. When Dr. Dain viewed them, he recognized the yellow pebbles as nuggets of almost pure gold. He questioned Captain

Sowers and the others and determined that the wagon trains had passed over a gold deposit, leaving behind tire marks etched in golden rock. The residents of the town of Yreka, California, became excited, and fourteen prospectors, including Dr. Dain, made plans to return in the spring and search the canyons adjoining the Black Rock Desert east of Granite Creek.

Paiute warriors attacked the Dain-led party while looking for gold and killed all but two members. The two survivors organized another party and searched the Black Rock Range for weeks, despite sporadic attacks by bands of Paiutes. They did not find the canyon of golden tracks left by the iron rims of the wagon train.

The dates of this story, and Dr. Dain's search of 1845, are suspect, because no one saw the yellow stones as gold until after the California Gold Rush four years later. The search took place sometime after 1850 if it occurred at all. Dain was a member of the Burney Party of 1864 that searched the Black Rock Desert. It was 1846 before any wagon trains traveled the Lassen Trail to California. The phrase "Blue Bucket Mine" appeared in print for the first time in 1869 in the *Portland Daily Bee*.

Harry S. Drago discovered through his research that in the 1920s, two young Californians arrived at Humboldt, Nevada, and bought burros, food and mining tools for a prospecting trip forty miles to the northwest of that town beginning at the eastern fringes of the Black Rock Desert. The two men were in the mountains for five weeks, and when their supplies were exhausted, they stumbled into the little desert hamlet of Jungo. The Jungo storekeeper stated that the two prospectors told him they were the grandsons of one of the members of the Sowers Party and were searching for the canyon of gold. Their late father had drawn a map of the area, and they began searching for it.

Their first attempt failed, and although they were exhausted, they were not disillusioned or discouraged and were determined to try again. Other descendants motivated by their ancestors' tales also searched the Black Rock Desert and canyons, concentrating on the twenty-one miles between Granite Peak to the south and Division Peak to the north, where the wagon train had traveled.

One of the later searchers in the 1930s and 1940s was Peter Organ, who searched the Black Rock, Santa Rosas and Jackson Mountains in Humboldt County, Nevada. He told Harry Drago after years of searching: "I know right where that gold is. I figure to get it next spring." He never found it.

In 1902, J.H. Murray, a cook for the Gerlach Land and Livestock Company, found ore on the west slope of Division Peak, known also as

Donnelly Mountain, in the Black Rock Range. The Donnelly Mining District includes the Rasser, Reeder, Jumbo and Tehoqua Mines, which began operations in 1911. George Austin discovered gold in the Jackson Range, and former president Herbert Hoover hoped to invest in the Iron King Mine after visiting it in 1936.

Prospectors have explored, at least on the surface, every draw and canyon in the area. They discovered ore in the Donnelly Mining District, which occurs in narrow veins of granite intruded with quartz and slate and varies in width from three inches to a maximum of two and a half feet. Drifting sand, a rock fall or a flash flood buried the gold vein. But what nature covers it eventually uncovers, and a lucky searcher in the Black Rock Range will find it when conditions are right.

SUMMARY

It is not surprising that the Blue Bucket Mine remains lost. The documented gold is only one or two small gold nuggets found on top of a gopher mound or in any one of dozens of unnamed creeks or washes in Eastern and Central Oregon. The nuggets found in the Camp Creek Valley are too small for the Blue Bucket gold, and the waggoneers never went farther east than four miles east of Camp Creek, eliminating both Scissors Creek and Spanish Gulch, located just east of Antone. Tiller and Clark recommend a thorough search along Clover Creek. Eugene Field of Burbank, Washington, followed the two authors' advice in 1971. He prospected both Clover and Leaflet Creek canyons on the north slope of Hampton Buttes and found nothing, which he noted in a letter to *Gold* magazine. The only mineral claim on Hampton Butte is not gold but a manganese prospect staked in 1931 by C.M. Gulovson at five thousand feet.

In a sense, the Blue Bucket Mine always remains lost. Anyone picking up a single gold nugget near water or at an unnamed dry wash could claim that he or she found the placer deposit. The search area can cover at least six Oregon counties, and evaluating the evidence anywhere west of the area searched by the Scientific Safari of 1958 is worth consideration. The wagon train entered the Harney Basin by way of the South Fork of Pine Creek. Lieutenant Dixon and a U.S. Army survey party discovered indications of gold there in 1859, where Jessie Harritt and the Meek Party camped on the night of September 5. But a year later, two parties searching for gold on Pine Creek discovered nothing. From this camp south to either Big Rock Creek or

East Cow Creek, the Lost Caravan entered the Harney Basin on September 6, heading west to camp at the mouth of Rattlesnake Creek.

Tracing the route of the Meek caravan, one discovers that the path never crossed an area where commercial gold mining occurs. The gold may lie on one of the side treks made by members of the Meek Party while looking for water or chasing cattle. On September 13, 1845, according to Jessie Harritt, the wagons "made a start and traveled three miles, met the men who accompanied the pilot [Meek] in search of water but found none. We returned to our old encampment and stopped for the night." This westward travel toward Tired Horse Lake and Sand Hollow or northwest to the ghost town of Stauffer was from their camp on Lost Creek, where it sinks into the ground at Sinking Hollows on the north side of Wagontire Mountain.

There are no gold discoveries at Lost Creek. Gold prospecting and later nitrate operations occurred in 1917. The American Nitrate Company did a large amount of prospected tunneling and quarrying on Wagontire Mountain for nitrates at points along Lost Creek and its radiating gulches about the southwest slope of the mountain.

The nitrates did not extend to any considerable depth, causing the abandonment of all mining operations. But the American Nitrate Company did not prospect on the western side of Wagontire Mountain. The gold may be lying on one of the overlooked western slopes of the mountain, where one of the Herren children dug a hole in a dry creek searching for water, or where streams have cut deep radiating gorges into the slopes of the mountain and into the sides of these gorges where there are exposures of rock. The gold picked up by a member or members of the Meek Party of 1845 was from a placer deposit. This means that the gold eroded from a quartz vein or from another gangue material like silicified country rock and was transported away from the main lode by the action of flowing water eons ago. In the Lost Cabin Mining District, ten miles north of Plush, rocks of rhyolitic flows filled with seams of clay and limonite exist along with quartz, including gold and copper-oxide minerals. These seams resemble the limonite seams on Wagontire Mountain.

The Blue Bucket Placer, if located to the north near Camp Creek and the Crooked River toward the Blue Mountains, would be like gold found in the isolated mining districts of Northeastern Oregon, such as the Spanish Gulch district, where there is a small exposure of pre-tertiary rocks in an area covered by tertiary lavas and sediments.

Other minerals that may be present are pyrite, chalcopyrite and galena in the original ore vein also containing gold. Upper Silver Creek, where

Zachariah Moreland found iron pyrites in a creek near Chicken Hawk Butte, which is not on modern maps, could be the lode rock source of the Blue Bucket Placer and, to the prospector, a source of lead, silver and other minerals.

Searchers can cite other reasons to look anywhere along the paths of one of the splinter parties where the Meek caravan traveled after splitting up at the GI Ranch, leading to the rediscovery of the site where one or two gold nuggets were found by the Meek-led train in 1845.

A modern searcher may discern the general path of the Meek caravan within a mile or two before their parting at GI Ranch and miss the gold discovery site by three hundred yards. After the site of the main separation of the two hundred wagons, the search area fans out even more from the east of Ant Creek and the north edge of Pringle Flat, north to Crooked River, and is the main reason that gold remains lost to this day. The only way to prove that the Blue Bucket Mine exists is to "show me the gold" in an area where the Meek caravan is known to have traveled during the summer of 1845, which has not occurred, in my view.

LOST CABIN MINES

FOLLOW THE PATH OF "SET-THEM-UP"

The Lost Cabin Mine keeps exclusive company as the subject of the second-oldest account of lost mine legends in Oregon. It falls closely behind folklore surrounding the Blue Bucket Placer. The story of the Lost Cabin Mine began in the winter of 1850, when a sixty-year-old miner arrived in the Northern California town of Yreka. He became a welcome sight in Yreka's dozen saloons and bars when he entered, shouting out, "Set them up for everyone" as he ordered. He then paid for everyone in the house. In fact, no one knew who the old miner was. He was known only as "Set-Them-Up," and the only information about him was that he had more than enough gold dust and nuggets to pay everyone's tab.

There were suspicions about his gold and where it came from, and this grabbed the attention of eavesdroppers. The secretive old miner would only hint that the source of his gold was a rich placer mine up north in the southwestern part of the Oregon Territory, where he had erected a small cabin. That spring, he left Yreka as quickly as the snow melted to trek back to his cabin and gold mine.

Set-Them-Up returned the next winter, in 1851, and bought his customary round of drinks for everyone. His generosity was as great as ever, and all the saloon patrons of Yreka were sorry to see him leave again the following spring for the North Country and anticipated his return for the winter. He failed to return to Yreka in 1852 and the winter after that. Bar patrons believed either that Native Americans killed him or that he died a natural death from a heart attack.

Yreka residents, believing that the old miner was either dead or missing, thought it would be right and proper to journey up north to Oregon and try to locate the placer mine. The missing miner had left behind hints about his mine's location, and experienced prospectors might be able to find it.

The party of Northern Californians journeyed north to Jacksonville, where gold discoveries had occurred at Rich Gulch on Jackson Creek in December 1851. The plan of these gold seekers was to lay low and find out any information on Set-Them-Up's mine. This plan went awry when one member of the party, after drinking too much and hearing talk in a Jacksonville saloon, told John W. Hillman, a twenty-year-old miner from Albany, New York, and other Oregon miners about their quest for a rich placer mine. The Californians tried but failed to sneak out of town before Hillman could organize a party to trail them out of Jacksonville when they left to prospect for what later became known as the original Lost Cabin Mine. Hillman's party consisted of Isaac G. Skeeters, George Ross, Henry Klippel, J.S. Louden, Pat McManus and five others.

The Californians headed north to the upper reaches of the Rogue River, and the Hillman group followed closely behind in a game of hide-and-seek. The Californians would rush through the brush, scatter, double back on their path, set up camp and leave with their campfires still burning in the middle of the night while secretly relocating to another camp, this time forgoing any campfires. This lasted until each group's food and supplies ran out. They then met and agreed to combine forces to hunt wild game and prospect together. After several days, the entire group of prospectors became lost.

Hillman had a solution to lead everyone back to civilization. He volunteered to lead a small group of able-bodied men to the summit of the nearest peak to locate their position. The party reached the top of the unknown ridge on June 12, 1853. Although they found no gold, they discovered a national treasure later known as Crater Lake. Hillman wrote fifty years later: "While riding up a long, sloping mountain we suddenly came in sight of water, and were very much surprised as we did not expect to see any lakes. I did not know but we had come in sight of, and close to, Klamath Lake, and not until my mule stopped within a few feet of the rim of Crater Lake did I look down, and if I had been riding a blind mule, I believe I would ride over the edge to death and destruction."

Hillman's party had little time to enjoy the scenery. They rolled boulders down the rim of the caldera, looking around for an outlet to the lake. Finding

Deep Blue Lake (Crater Lake), discovered by prospector John Hillman while searching for the Lost Cabin Mine. *Photo by author, circa 1962.*

none, they voted to name it Deep Blue Lake over second-place Mysterious Lake and other choices. The recombined prospecting party returned to Jacksonville. Their discovery of Crater Lake remained unknown, as they returned without finding any gold.

There is an alternative explanation why Set-Them-Up never returned to Yreka. The old miner may have been the first to discover gold on Daisy Creek in Southwest Oregon in 1850. He later returned during the spring of 1851, as soon as new gold discoveries occurred in December 1851 or January 1852 that triggered a large influx of miners. The horde of miners and merchants erected a mining camp that later became the town of

Steve Oester, Southern Oregon prospector. *Southern Oregon Historical Society #000450.*

Jacksonville, Oregon. By March, claims were dotting the entire gulch. As a result, old Set-Them-Up either worked out or ran off from his claim and so had no reason to return to Yreka. He might have whooped it up in the saloons of Jacksonville, the first target of the group of Californians who tried to trace his trail.

Another searcher for the Lost Cabin Mine was Steve Oester, who came to Jacksonville and had his picture taken at the famous Peter Britt studio. Oester must have had good reasons to believe that the lost mine was in the Steamboat Mountain area on the upper Applegate River, where he searched for over seven years. Oester, nicknamed "Oyster," staked a claim, Hungry Placer, on Thompson Creek and used the placer's meager earnings to finance a grubstake to allow him to prospect for the Lost Cabin Mine.

Oester's search in the Steamboat Mountain area made good sense. This mountainous area had eight lode claims and a placer claim discovered in 1860. In addition, there is a question as to why Set-Them-Up would journey so far up the Rogue River when gold existed in the Siskiyou Mountains twenty miles south of Jacksonville, instead of going forty miles to the north in the Crater Lake region.

The only placer gold from the upper Rogue River area found by gold panners was on Elk Creek and traced upstream, leading to the discovery of the Al Sarena Mine in 1897. This placer, bypassed by the Hillman Party of 1853, does not fit Set-Them-Up's description of his rich placer deposit or the Lost Cabin Mine. And there is another reason to consider the Steamboat Mountain area as the site of the Lost Cabin Mine, found in 1870 and lost again.

John Hayes told Dale Vincent of the *Oregonian* in 1948 how his father, Bill, a blacksmith at Rock Point stage station, knew two men, Constantine Magruder and Doc Lee, who found an abandoned cabin and a pan of gold nuggets during a deer hunting trip in 1870.

On the second day out of their hometown of Central Point, where Magruder owned a store, the pair set up camp on a little spring on one of the gulches in the Steamboat Mountains. About noon the next day, Magruder, who was hunting alone at the time, noticed the remains of a broken-down and deserted cabin hidden in a grove of trees and thick brush. The curious Magruder dismounted from his horse and made his way through the undergrowth and into the cabin, which had collapsed except for the front wall of logs and the attached remains of the roof. In the center of the doorway, a ten-inch-diameter fir was growing, establishing that the cabin had seen no use since the growth of the tree.

Above: Constantine Magruder's Store, Central Point. Magruder and Doc Lee discovered and lost the legendary Lost Cabin Mine. *Southern Oregon Historical Society #0043.*

Left: Gold scales used throughout the Old West. *From* River of No Return *by Robert G. Bailey, 1947. Author's copy.*

Magruder squeezed through the doorway and past the tree and sat down until his eyes adjusted to the dim light. First, the storekeeper noticed an old pick handle partly rotted off and a rusted gold pan covered with debris. He then scraped the needles and leaves away from the gold pan and found a pile of gold nuggets lying in the center.

It was not until dusk that Magruder made it back to camp and showed the nuggets he had pocketed to Doc Lee, who was cooking the last of their food over a campfire. They figured the rich placer deposit must be close to the decaying cabin, which was one day's travel from their campsite, and they hoped to search the next day. But the next morning they realized they had to head home, as they had failed to kill any deer and were out of food. On arriving at Central Point, they showed the gold nuggets to Bill Hayes, the blacksmith and father of John Hayes, who knew mineralogy. Hayes offered to go into partnership with Lee and Magruder, and they accepted, because they needed an expert on mining.

The three men returned the next week. Lee and Magruder could not locate their old deer-hunting campsite after one week of searching. Somehow, they became lost, and without this landmark, Magruder could not track his path back to the old cabin. The three men searched gulch after gulch until their supplies ran out. They returned, prospecting until 1875, when the partnership broke up.

Was this the lost cabin of the old miner Set-Them-Up? The cabin and date fit the description, and it is the closest anyone has come to finding a lost miner's cabin in the wilderness of Southwestern Oregon. The ten-inch-diameter tree would now be three to four feet in diameter if it is still standing and if no forest fires have swept through the area. Certainly, all traces of the old cabin are gone, since it was decaying in 1870.

Using the phrase "lost mine" for the Steamboat Mountain area is a misnomer. The term *steamboat* in this context comes from the mining term *steam-boating*, which refers to a mine that has run out of ore or does not live up to expectations. Steve Oester, who searched Thompson Creek, the Steve Fork and Orster Creek, and another prospector, Jim Carberry, who searched Carberry Creek, could not find the Lost Cabin Mine. And the threesome of Doc Lee, Constantine Magruder and Bill Hayes did not stumble across it over a five-year search. The Lost Cabin Mine is undiscovered in the wild and rough terrain of Southwestern Oregon.

The Wilson Brothers Gold

Theodore Harper found a willing drinking partner in Samuel L. Simpson when both men lived for weeks at the Carr House in Portland in 1870. On a rainy night common to Western Oregon, Ted Harper called on Simpson, who was in the process of closing his law practice in Corvallis, since he was making little money at it. The few hundred dollars Simpson had saved he spent on rent, food and mostly drink.

Samuel L. Simpson, obituary photo from the *Oregon Law Annual*, 1899. Poet, newspaperman and author of "The Lost Cabin Mine," an article that first appeared in 1872 in *Overland Monthly. Courtesy of the Oregon Historical Society.*

Arriving at Simpson's office, Harper took the chair Simpson offered and parked his tall frame in the seat near the stove and said, "It's a nasty night for April."

"It is indeed," Simpson replied, stooping to put more wood in the stove. "And you need to dry yourself off." Simpson later wrote accounts of his meetings and trek with Harper in the *Oregonian* and *Overland Monthly* in 1872.

"Yes, I had some difficulty in finding your office," said Harper. "This reminds me that I did not come here to discuss the weather, but to talk business. I have come here to share with you a valuable secret and to solicit your assistance in a project which if successfully prosecuted, will enrich us both."

Simpson became uneasy, because Harper offered a proposal to commit larceny or, worse yet, draw him into armed robbery. Simpson knew Harper only from their nights drinking together in Portland saloons and a brief stay at the Carr House. All Simpson had learned was that Harper had lived in Chicago in the late 1850s and had relatives in San Francisco.

"No, it is all legal," said Harper, sensing Simpson's nervous twitch. "I only ask of you for the confidence I am about to tell you is a pledge of secrecy in the event that you do not join me in the project to which I have alluded."

Simpson consented to listen to Harper, who suggested they first lock the door. After Simpson got up to lock the door, Harper lighted a cigar and asked, "Did you ever hear the story of 'The Lost Cabin Mine'? I did not think you did. Here is the last letter from my cousin James Wilson that you should read":

San Francisco, Oct. 26, 1859.
Dear cousin,
I had hoped to see you before this, but the end has come sooner than I expected. I dreamed of that cabin in the wilds of Oregon, last night, and saw poor Harry fall again before the cowardly Shasta Natives; and it is nearly over. I must write what I intended to have spoken, and endeavor to

*give you such directions as will enable you to find it, Theodore, and enjoy
its hidden gold. The first part of your course is plain enough; Start from
Jacksonville and keep to the California road for* [Yreka].

From a series of letters Harper received from his cousin James Wilson, he
was able to tell Simpson during the spring of 1853, when the Rogue Indian
War broke out, that his two cousins, the brothers James and Harry Wilson,
had arrived at the mining camp of Jacksonville. They assembled a small
party of experienced miners fully supplied to prospect for gold along the
rivers and broken range of mountains southeast of the mining camp. The
party was out for weeks, having little success, when one of the miners lost his
life in a skirmish with Native Americans.

A council was held at a mineral spring whose bitter-tasting water stained
the rocks over which it flowed from its start at a tall boulder shaped like a
crude hourglass. All the searchers except the Wilson brothers decided to
return to Jacksonville and wait for the war to be over. They agreed that the
Wilson brothers should have the largest share of the group's provisions and
ammunition, which they would need to continue their search. The others
would retrace their steps by the shortest and safest route back to Jacksonville.

"Goodbye, men and good luck to you," said James Wilson, swinging up
in his stirrups and holding his rifle aloft. "There is gold out there beyond the
line of mountains, and we're going to dig it out. We will come back rich as
kings or die trying."

The departing miners never saw the brothers again. They reached
Jacksonville after days of cautious travel, waiting in vain for any news about
the Wilsons. Continuing his story, Harper was able to tell Simpson that his
cousins had traveled beyond the range of hostile tribes. They had reached
a green and narrow valley surrounded by mountains where a snow-fed
stream flowed over smooth and shining pebbles. Here they intended to rest
themselves and their pack mules while they leisurely prospected for gold
in the valley. They constructed a log cabin interspaced with gun holes as
protection for themselves and their equipment against any marauders.

Henry Wilson, on the morning after their arrival, began to fell trees to
build their small fortress on the edge of the woods near the stream. James set
forth, walking slowly, rifle in hand, to hunt game.

At 10:00 a.m., he killed a deer, which he carried back to camp. He reached
the little stream sweating and thirsty. He set the carcass down on a pebbly
bar and stooped to get a drink. Just as his lips touched the freezing water,
his eyes caught the glisten of yellow metal scattered among the gravel of the

Mining town of Jacksonville, Oregon, circa 1860, looking northeast, where Samuel L. Simpson and Ted Harper began their quest for the Lost Cabin Mine in 1867. *Southern Oregon Historical Society No. 02735.*

creek bottom. Henry dropped flat on the ground to examine the sandy earth on which he had stood. There was gold everywhere!

Henry yelled in such loud joy that it brought his brother James bursting across the small valley. Working together, they finished their cabin the next day and began panning for gold. It took only two weeks to scour out all the easy placer gold from the stream, and they began to plan their return to civilization.

The brothers thought it prudent to remain in this valley of gold until the Rogue Indian War was over, waiting while the white settlers, miners and soldiers under the command of Brigadier General Joseph Lane drove the Native Americans from Southwestern Oregon. The pair made an excavation in the center of the cabin floor and lined it with rock. Into this vault they deposited their gold dust and nuggets in bags of tanned deerskin in case an attack forced them to flee, leaving the heavy gold sacks concealed in a vault.

No attack came in the next three weeks, so on one sunny morning they agreed it was time to return to Jacksonville. They gathered their horses, which had grown plump and vigorous on the bountiful pasture. Unexpectedly, twenty Shasta warriors appeared, followed by a war cry from above the stream bank forty yards from the cabin. Henry, who was in front of James and leading two of the horses, fell with a loud thud and mournful groan, his two horses rearing and falling at the same time. The Shasta tribe burst forth from their forest cover and rushed forward, screaming battle cries with great fury.

James emptied his rifle with superb accuracy and then drew his revolver. The warriors quickly ran out of ammunition and retreated to the cover of the stream bank to reload. James saw his only chance of survival. He leapt onto the back of the only horse that remained uninjured, and it was beyond rifle range. It took him ten seconds to career down the valley, rifle bullets zinging all around him. The war party, now on foot because of their injured horses, could not give chase quickly enough to catch him.

James reached the frontier settlements after a journey of incredible hardship. He booked passage to San Francisco to obtain further medical treatment. Afterward, he started writing to his cousin Ted Harper, who lived in Chicago at that time. In the fall of 1859, Harper received news of James's death and received a bundle of papers, among them James's final, unfinished letter to him, which he later shared with Simpson.

"That is all I know about it," said Harper. "And here is my proposition: Let us jointly provision an outfit and spend the summer in the mountains of Southern Oregon. With the clew we have I verily believe we shall find the cabin."

"I am with you," Simpson said as he shook his hand.

They talked over the details of the expedition until dawn. It would be the middle of May before the snow melted and the rivers were passable. It would take two months before all the preparations would be complete. They would both need to buy a saddle horse, two pack animals and supplies for six months before they could travel to Jacksonville. From there, it would be onward to the southeast to locate the hourglass-shaped rock where the Wilson brothers had separated from their main party.

Then there was the inkblot on the unfinished letter. What was James Wilson trying to write? Simpson had looked at the unfinished letter for at least the tenth time and finally sat in a rocker, reading it dreamily with a lead pencil in his hand. He so desired more details. Later, Simpson wrote that he yearned for a spirit hand to seize the pencil and complete the letter.

In the rocker, Simpson drifted into a dreamlike sleep. In his dream, he pictured a shadow of a man, tall, muscular and with a brown face and bushy beard. The supernatural presence wore a miner's gray flannel shirt, no coat and with a revolver belted to his side. Simpson could not move or speak. The ghost of Harry Wilson looked at Harper, who was napping in a chair across the room. Then the apparition looked toward Simpson with sad and sympathetic eyes. Simpson woke up and picked the letter off the floor, waking Harper, who got up and put wood in the stove.

In the blank spot below the inkblot, there was a new added feature in pencil. It seemed to represent two ranges of mountains intercepting each other at right angles. In the center of the rectangular space on the lower side was a small diagram resembling the large one in shape. It was the representation of a miner's pick. At that moment, Simpson could not make out the mysterious symbolism before him and decided not to mention to Harper the dream and the addition to the drawing.

Simpson began to reread the letter in the drawing below the inkblot. He noted that there was a range of mountains running north and south, intersecting at right angles with another range through which a gold seeker must pass. There to the south, the mystic emblem of the pick marked the location of the vault of gold! Simpson turned to Harper with this interpretation of the secret, and Harper, too, became ecstatic.

The southeast direction of travel by way of the Portland-to-Sacramento stage line encompassed a hopelessly wide path. The Wilson party undoubtedly had departed from the stage road to avoid any encounters with Native Americans. The prospectors would have to travel where the geological terrain was favorable to the mining of gold, which would be that part of the Western Cascade Mountains east of Emigrant Creek to Keene Creek.

The question lingers about the truth of the story and the content Simpson added. The Lost Cabin Mine first appeared in the magazine *Overland Monthly* in November 1872 and the *Oregonian* on November 3, 1872, later reprinted in the September 1900 issue of the magazine *Oregon Native Son* as a memorial to Simpson. The story was presented as fact. But it included fictional elements.

Least among these fictional aspects is that Simpson never had a law office in Portland. He practiced law first in Salem after passing the bar in 1867, and the next year he moved to Albany and finally to Corvallis. His clients were few, and he never liked the profession. Simpson retired in April 1870, abandoning the practice of law about the same time as the Harper visit. He bought the *Corvallis Gazette* and became its editor. This paper failed, and Simpson then became the editor of the *Oregon State Journal* in March 1871. He also received a $150-a-month salary from Hugh Bancroft for contributing to Bancroft's book *The History of the Pacific Coast*.

Writers attribute the supernatural encounter with the ghost of Harry Wilson to an alcoholic stupor, but it is a dramatic literary device. W.W. Fidler described Simpson in the 1916 *Oregon Historical Quarterly* as "the most drunken poet, and the most poetical drunkard that ever made the muses smile or weep" and as "brilliant, but alcoholic and undependable" as a reporter. But the twenty-five-year-old Simpson had at least twenty years of sobriety ahead of him before he died in 1899 from a drunken fall on a Portland sidewalk.

The Lost Cabin story was too good for Simpson to forget, especially as a young journalist struggling to begin his writing career. He had recently completed, in July 1868, what would become his most famous poem, "Beautiful Willamette," and was desperate for new subjects. It is possible that Simpson met Harper and heard the Lost Cabin story directly from him or from someone else during the time he resided at the Carr House in Portland. Simpson had to end the story, and he did so by inventing a piece of journalism in which the writer becomes part of the story one hundred years before Hunter S. Thompson invented the style and the term *gonzo journalism*.

Simpson wrote in 1872 that he and Harper made the trek south to Jacksonville. Then traveling southeast, they found an hourglass-shaped boulder with a mineral spring at its base. From there, they journeyed for a while and endured difficult travel to discover and then climb a lofty peak. They used a telescope to sweep the unknown country to view the north–south range of mountains intersecting at right angles through which the men had already passed. Incredibly, this pass matched the drawing below the inkblot!

They then went forward with dreams filled with future riches and lives in which nothing would impede their progress. They entered a narrow valley walled by steep mountains bordered on each side by a beautiful stream. As they walked in the forest, they found a square, black object half buried in a tangle of weeds. It was the remains of the Lost Cabin, containing nothing but an empty pen of scorched and blackened logs.

Simpson took a pick from one of the packs and stepped into the weed-choked enclosure. Bending the weeds aside, Simpson found a human skull and the remains of Harry Wilson. The Shasta Indigenous people had intended to burn the cabin to the ground, but only the drier roof shingles burned, leaving the lower green logs intact. Simpson struck the pick into the ground near the center of the cabin, lifted it and drove the long wedge of iron to the handle into the loose soil.

The point of the pick clanged against metallic material. At the same time, Harper uttered a cry of mortal anguish and collapsed at Simpson's feet as a rifle accidentally discharged. Simpson ended the story by describing himself falling into a daze due to the shock of Harper's mishap, the excitement of the search and finding the remains of Wilson. Simpson wrote in November

Above: Siskiyou Summit stagecoach, which picked up Samuel L. Simpson near the Oregon border in 1867. *From* History of the Oregon Country *by Harvey Scott, 1924, author's copy.*

Left: Last of Southern Oregon stage drivers. *From* History of the Oregon Country *by Harvey Scott, 1924, authors' copy.*

GROUP OF STAGE DRIVERS AT ASHLAND, OREGON, IN 1887

Names, sitting: on left, "Ab" Geddings; on right, Dan Cawley; standing: beginning on left, Nort Eddings, Charles Laird, "Hank" Geddings, George Chase, probably Buck Montgomery (with gun, Wells Fargo express messenger). The name of the man on the extreme right is unknown

1872 that a stagecoach driver found him "nude and tan, gibbering like a monkey and harmless as a baby" near the Oregon-California boundary line and immediately dispatched him north to Portland.

In his story, Simpson left the impression that the shot killed Harper, but in the San Francisco city directory, Theo Harper is working as a carpenter in 1875. Neither man had found the lost vault of gold, nor did Simpson return to look for it—if he ever made the search in the first place.

Simpson did make a trip to Southern Oregon to tour the Oregon Caves soon after their discovery in 1874 to gather material for a magazine article. The article was too full of fiction, according to biographer W.W. Fidler, "to be of any worth as the description of the place, and hardly worthy of the author of 'The Lost Cabin'."

During 1874, for the first time in years, Simpson was in a sober state, and this continued for the entire winter, as there was no alcohol anywhere in the Coastal Mountains. He became destitute, unable to buy even a plug of tobacco though he craved it intensely. If the impoverished Simpson knew where the Lost Cabin Mine and Vault was located and could separate fact from fiction, he would have certainly searched again while in Southern Oregon for the gold as well as material for another story.

The description Simpson gives about the Lost Cabin Mine corresponds closely to history and geography, although he exaggerates the distances he and Harper allegedly traveled. Whether this was a coincidence or based on the facts from James Wilson's letters is unknown. The area of the volcanic lands of the Western Cascades east from Emigrant Creek and ten miles east to Keene Creek is a favorable geological location for the occurrence of gold. Going directly east, a prospector must travel one hundred miles to find gold in the High-Grade District of Lake County. The lofty peak Simpson mentions is the one he climbed in his imagination with Harper, likely Soda Mountain.

Soda Mountain, at 6,091 feet, in Jackson County, is the highest mountain in the area and conforms to the lofty peak in Simpson's narrative where the two mountain ranges, the north–south Cascades and the west–east Siskiyou Mountains, intersect at right angles. The Barron Gold Mine is located eight miles southeast of Ashland and ten miles north of the California-Oregon border at 3,450 feet. Hydrothermally altered lavas and tuffs with sulfides are the host rocks occurring with wire silver and realgar.

The Barron lode deposit could be the source of the placer gold and nuggets that the Wilson brothers completely panned out of Sampson Creek. That, Fisher Creek or a side creek are the closest sources of water near the Barron Mine. Rogue River Indians killed prospector Granville Keene in 1856 on the banks of Keene Creek, which was later named for the prospector, proving that hostile Native Americans patrolled the area in the early 1850s where the Wilson brothers traveled.

Another prominent landmark is Pilot Rock (elevation 5,910 feet), a volcanic plug rising above the Rogue River valley and visible from forty miles away from the Shasta Valley. This could also be the landmark Simpson refers to.

Gravestone of poet and journalist Samuel L. Simpson, Lone Fir Cemetery, Portland, Oregon. *Photo by author.*

The area where the vault of gold and the Lost Cabin Mine is located, if the Simpson narrative is correct, is northwest of Soda Mountain near Sampson Creek, south of Mount McLoughlin.

THE THREE-SIDED CABIN MINE

In the early 1860s, two Frenchmen found a source of gold close to where they had built a three-sided log cabin abutting a stone cliff. In one year, they successfully mined $50,000 worth of gold. Local pioneer merchants sold supplies to the Frenchmen and, during long talks, determined the general location of the Frenchmen's mine. On more than one occasion, the pair showed Elijah Bristow, the pioneer settler of Pleasant Hill, the gold they had mined. The Frenchmen also stopped at the nearby farm of Thomas Hunsaker to get their mules shod when returning from their mine. Bristow said that they turned at the old military road near Coal Creek to get to their mine. He may have been the first searcher for the mine when he hunted on the prairie later named for him. Bristow found no trace of the cabin and gave up. There are rumors that the Frenchmen buried a pot of gold under one corner of the cabin.

Other early settlers saw the two French miners along the Central Military Road between Eugene and Risdon Ranch. Occasionally, they would buy supplies at Cottage Grove and Klamath Falls. Hunsaker said they took the steep Bristow Trail starting at Campers Flat, which traversed the ridge between Coal Creek, which flows north into the Middle Fork of the Willamette, and Indian Creek, which is six miles up to Bristow Meadows in the high country. Where they went from that point, no one could say.

The two Frenchmen carried their gold on their return trip on pack animals and transported it over secret trails until they reached the Coast Fork of the Willamette River, passing the Bristow homestead at Pleasant Hill following the wagon road into Eugene City. The Eugene bankers were unable at that time to obtain enough paper money to purchase all the gold. This forced the duo to take their gold to San Francisco, where the banks had more monetary reserves.

The two miners stayed over and spent a whole winter at San Francisco. By spring, they were destitute, deciding to return to their mine in Oregon by way of Klamath Falls as soon as the mountain roads were passable. They hired a Native American woman from the Klamath Reservation to cook and clean for them and transported her by mule to their mine.

She ran away during the summer of 1866 or 1867 because of the mental and physical abuse she suffered at the hands of the two Frenchmen. She told her story to soldiers working at Corral Springs on the Military Road from Eugene to old Fort Klamath. Corral Springs is located five miles northwest of Chemult and three miles west of US Highway 97.

The two Frenchmen then lived inside a three-sided enclosure, two sides formed by two large Douglas fir trees that fell in such a manner that their tops crossed forty feet in front of the cabin, forming a horse corral against a straight rocky wall that served as the rear wall of the enclosure. The sluice box was located a short distance from the cabin. They pastured their horses on a prairie or meadow seen from the top rocky wall behind the cabin.

As soon as the Native American woman reached her home on the Klamath Indian reservation, she told her brother how she suffered at the hands of the two Frenchmen. He became angered, demanding she take him and three other warriors back to the mine. She was able to show her brother and tribal members who joined the search only where the Frenchmen had departed from the military road.

Fortunately for her, after days of searching, the party found the mine. On arriving, they worked out a plan of attack. They waited until the Frenchmen were inside and trapped, then made a direct frontal attack on the cabin started by a war cry. The Frenchmen rushed through the door with their guns blazing, trying to reach the cover of the two large fallen logs that lay in front of the house. They failed, and the warriors shot them dead.

Then the woman's brother told his band that he would kill any of them if they dared return to the mine. But he never prohibited them talking about the incident to locals and merchants, as he took immense pride in how he took revenge on his sister's behalf. His reputation was so fierce, and his character so admired for keeping his vows, that no Klamath tribesmen would do anything more than talk about the mine and his heroics. The band's members hoped to return to the mine or serve as guides for prospectors after the brother died, but he outlived them all, not dying until 1924, almost fifty-seven years after the attack.

William Page, who ran a tavern near the Klamath Indian Agency, heard the story directly from tribal members in 1906 or 1907. Page told the story to Thomas Hunsaker of Lowell, Oregon. Hunsaker originally heard the story from a Klamath County ranch hand named Hale in 1879 or 1880 and kept a journal about Southern Oregon history. Although the stories are thirty years apart, they match. When Hunsaker compared the two entries in his journal, they were the same.

Oregon Journal writer Randall S. Jones first heard about the story in 1924 from Al A. Reiner, a local guide from Oakridge. Reiner built a cabin at the mouth of Coal Creek on the Middle Fork of the Willamette at Campers Flat in the early 1920s. He guided parties over the summers, including Mr. Morton, an Englishman, and his wife, to Bristow Meadows to search for the mine.

Morton claimed to have a map pointing the way to the lost mine. Reiner never saw it. The Englishman prospected while Morton constructed a cabin on Ranger Prairie just northwest of Bristow Prairie. The fifty-five-year-old Morton was an experienced camper from Grays Harbor, Washington, and a former ship's carpenter by trade. At the end of the first summer, Morton

Al A. Reiner, a Cascade Mountain guide, circa 1920, escorting the Morton family near the rumored location of the Three-Sided Cabin Mine. *From* Treasure Hunting Northwest *by Ruby El Hult, 1971.*

and the Englishman departed the high country. Morton returned the next year accompanied by a Grays Harbor mail carrier, his wife and their five small children.

Reiner learned that Morton had a profitable business going. The English couple and the mail carrier had paid Morton all the expenses for the trip. This way, Morton got someone to help him prospect and finance his trip to the mountains while he completed his cabin.

The next year, Morton could not persuade anyone to pay for his trip to Ranger Prairie. He hired Reiner for the third year in a row to pack supplies. Reiner was amazed at the completed cabin. It measured forty feet by twenty feet square with a large stone fireplace at one end and was lined with tin to make it rat-proof. The cabin was a structure of artisanship in the middle of the wilderness.

Morton continued his solitary search for the mine. He finally told Reiner that he found it and proudly showed off a human leg bone said to be from one of the Frenchmen. He also found a magnesium deposit less than two miles from his large cabin, where he had built himself a smaller, second cabin.

Reiner guided other lost mine seekers to Bristow Meadows carrying rods and metal detectors. Others searched for prospect holes, a well-traveled trail or an old corral—anything left behind by the Frenchmen. One party found blackened stones, believing they were from an old fireplace. They dug around the fire site, hoping to find that rumored pot of gold buried in the corner of the cabin. Reiner insisted that the stones were only the remains of an ancient campfire.

One thing is certain. The Lost Frenchmen Mine is not at Bristow Meadows or Ranger Prairie, prospected by Morton and others throughout the years. Thomas Vaughn of Lane County believed the correct prairie is Lost Cabin Prairie just west of Bristow Prairie, where he located an old cabin in the 1930s. The log foundation is still visible, and the prairie and old lake bed are pocked with prospect holes. Vaughn never heard of anyone getting the gold or finding the mine.

To make matters more confusing, Frank X. Domphier, a resident of Oakridge since 1906, told the *Lane County Reporter* after reading Thomas Vaughn's story in 1958: "I have hunted every foot of Lost Cabin Prairie. I have never seen a cabin on it or a sign of where a cabin may have been. And the holes he calls prospect holes are just beaver holes."

Domphier commented on mining taking place on Johnson Meadows, named in honor of Bohemia Johnson. "Not right at Johnson Meadows, but about a mile from it. I remember a trench someone had dug in the side of the mountain. There were old shovels, picks and things lying around there. I packed dirt for two miles from there in a packsack. Three trips I made, and washed out the dirt, and I never got any color."

A California miner discovered the Johnson Meadows Mine after he trekked from Oakridge to ten miles east of the town to a little pine opening. From here, he hired the elderly Jap Hills to pack his supplies to Johnson Meadows. After Hills got too old to pack, the Californian hired Al Reiner to pack him in and out from Camper Flat.

The Californian gave up mining for the season when his tunnel caved in and he realized that it would take all summer to clear it. The next year, he showed up with his teenage son in the hopes that his son could help him move the debris and allow the teenager to continue the mining operation. After a month, they abandoned the mine. "I've taken out enough to last me the rest of my life and keep him the rest of his life, too, so we decided to just go back to California," the miner told Reiner.

Reiner returned to Johnson Meadows years later and saw a trail running to a bluff at the mouth of a small creek. About thirty feet up on the bluff there were signs of digging and a collapsed tunnel. Reiner never sought the Two Frenchmen Mine. He invoked a theory after talking with Morton,

Hunsaker and the California miner, as well as other treasure hunters over the years in the Bohemian Mining District.

The Bristow, Ranger and Johnson Meadows area drains to the northwest into the Steamboat Creek headwaters, where placer gold occurs. In addition, to the north of Steamboat Creek headwaters lies the rich Bohemian mining district, where the mine dumps on Champion Creek are visible with binoculars from the high meadows. In addition, the three southeastern mines of the Bohemia District—Mayflower, Riverside and Oregon-Colorado—are even closer to the high meadows.

Bohemia Johnson discovered gold near the head of City Creek in 1863, and a mile or two to the east is the Mayflower Mine on Horse Heaven Creek, between 3,000 and 3,400 feet elevation. The creek flows south to Steamboat Creek. Horse Heaven Creek begins near Horse Heaven Meadows in the Calapooya Mountains, a spur range of the Cascades. There is a natural pasture where miners and prospectors fed their stock and turned loose their horses and mules without worry that they would stray. It also fits the description of the meadow given by the two Frenchmen. All they had to do to avoid trackers was travel the longer way south to Camper Flat and then west to Bristow Meadows over the Calapooya Mountain divide, then to Horse Heaven Creek. They would then head north, upstream, to reach their three-sided cabin and nearby mine and cabin at or near Horse Heaven Meadows.

THE CASCADES

W.A. Paul's Map

William August Paul, a Linn County pioneer, gave David Smith a map showing the location of a gold ledge on an unnamed butte lying south of the Little North Santiam River near Elkhorn. Smith obtained the map sometime after he migrated to Oregon from Missouri in 1852 with his parents. Paul discovered this quartz ledge while hunting within sight of Mount Jefferson and returned with a sample that assayed $5,000 to the ton. He was later unable to locate his find, continued to search in vain and later passed on information to his son William S. Paul and George C. King.

The first gold discovered in what was to become the Little North Santiam Mining District was located four hundred feet north of the Little North Santiam River at Henline Creek, immediately below the cliffs of Henline Mountain, in 1872. In addition, William McKinney ten years earlier found a gold nugget worth $5.00 at the mouth of McKinney Creek. The McKinney discovery motivated Smith, twenty-six, to search for the gold source marked on his map. In 1873, Smith, who read the Bible, followed a Native American trail to the 4,389-foot summit of an unnamed mountain, stating, "This is as near to heaven as I'll ever get."

As Smith rode on his mule, named Nig, he named the peak Mount Horeb after the Egyptian mountain mentioned in the Old Testament. Following the map, Smith passed streams, ledges and rocks along the Native American trail. The last important landmark was twin rocks so close together that a rider and his mule could barely squeeze between them. Smith was enthused to find the twin rocks at the place indicated on his map.

Although he thoroughly prospected the area beyond the twin rocks, he failed to find the golden ledge. He made more trips to Mount Horeb, from his land claim located four miles east of Scio, to search for the ledge, but every trip ended in failure. Smith gave up the search after twelve years and moved to Lebanon, Oregon, and later to Portland, where he was still living in 1928. He had prospected too far south and at too high an elevation to find the golden ledge, which may exist on the northern slopes of Mount Horeb.

Mount Horeb lies immediately south of the North Santiam Mining District, the most rugged of all the gold-bearing areas of the Cascade Mountains, a result of recent lava flows and fragmented rocks. The first gold claim staked there, the Capital claim, was located four miles north of Mount Horeb. This occurred one year before Smith prospected the area. Later, twenty-five claims dotted the district, including the Oro, Black Eagle, Blue Jay, Ruth, Silver Star, Santiam, Riverside, Gold Bug, Bimetallic, Helvetia, Wolz, Silver King, Columbia, Copper, Mineral Harbor, Amalgamated and Gold Creek claims.

The claims of the Crown Mining & Milling Company are closest to David Smith's area of search on his map, located only two and one-quarter miles northeast of Mount Horeb at a three-thousand-foot elevation. The ten Crown claims are not at the ledge on Smith's map, because they are located on the northeast side of Elkhorn Mountain at the three-thousand-foot elevation across from Elkhorn Creek and not on Mount Horeb. The Crown Mine consists of exposed veins of quartz-diorite of undetermined shape. The U.S. Department of the Interior recommended in 1938 that prospecting might reveal string-like gold like those found at the Ogle Mountain Mine, located in the outlying sections of the North Santiam Mining District.

Today, the six-mile road to the summit of Mount Horeb begins four miles east of the community of Gates and terminates at a microwave tower. The location of the twin rocks on the old Native American trail may be at the Phantom Bridge, which is five miles east of Mount Horeb, but its location never led Smith to the gold prospect. Smith never found gold at the Mineral Harbor prospect above Stony Creek, northeast of Mount Horeb. The best chance to find an exposed vein of quartz-diorite like the Crown claims or gold stringers using modern geological techniques is from 500 feet above the main creeks of the Santiam Mining District, where all prospects occur upward to the 3,000-foot elevation contour, 1,300 feet lower than the summit of Mount Horeb.

George C. King of San Jose, California, and Robert L. Smith, two prospectors over eighty years of age, looked for William A. Paul's prospect during the first two weeks of August 1908. The two octogenarians, accompanied by W.S. Paul, the son of the original seeker, trekked from the home of the younger Paul at Crabtree to about thirty miles northwest of Detroit, the terminus of the Corvallis & Eastern Railroad. The threesome came across a mine on Ogle Mountain. From the descriptions of the terrain given to him by his father, the junior Paul believed this was the long-lost mine. David Smith had his map inverted and should have searched north on Ogle Mountain instead of on the southern unnamed peak shown on the map that he named Mount Horeb. If Smith had been on the correct peak, he would have found gold to the north on Ogle Mountain thirty years before the development of the Ogle Mountain Mine began in 1903.

THE MYSTERY MINE

James Johnson acquired his nickname, "Bohemia," from his place of birth in the German state of Bohemia. Johnson filed a gold claim thirty-five miles southwest of Cottage Grove in the Calapooya Mountains and named it the Mystery. When he died, he left behind other mysteries. Bohemia Johnson first headed to the gold territory in the Calapooya Mountains, a spur of the Cascade Mountains, when he was eluding arrest for either shooting or killing a Native American in Roseburg.

Killing a Native American was not a serious crime in the early 1860s. The penalty consisted of paying a small fine or spending four days in jail. But Johnson did not have the money and did not want to spend time in jail, so he left town and was able to return in the spring of 1863. He then enlisted the help of his prospecting partner, George Ramsey, to look for gold in the North Umpqua River. Together, they traced the gold colors upstream to Steamboat Creek and then to the head of City Creek. There the hungry Johnson killed a deer. While dressing the animal, he saw the glitter of crumbled gold quartz on the ground. It did not take him long to unearth specimens and determine that the ground was rich with fine, free gold.

In their excitement, Johnson and Ramsey climbed the 5,960-foot summit of an unnamed peak, later named Bohemia Mountain, to determine the quickest route to Johnson's hometown. They saw the Row River valley and headed toward the assay office in Cottage Grove. After arriving, they started a gold rush when they announced they had found gold. Within two years,

A.W. Redman wading for placer gold on south-flowing Steamboat Creek, ten miles south of the Bohemian Mining District. *Author's photo, circa 1962.*

Arrastre, a very crude and one of the earliest methods of pulverizing free-gold quartz for the release of the precious metal. The wheel in the foreground is an overshot water wheel which furnished the power for the mill. The ore was ground by hooking chains to hard rocks and dragging the latter in a circle over the gold ore until it was fine enough for the quartz and gold to be separated.

Arrastre for crushing gold. *From River of No Return by Robert G. Bailey, 1947, author's copy.*

more than one hundred claims were filed, including the one by Bird Farrier, who came to Oregon in 1845 and befriended Johnson after Johnson first visited the Bohemia Mining District in 1865.

In the fall of 1867, Bird Farrier made the first sale of mining property in the Bohemia District when he sold what is now known as the Excelsior Claim, on the summit of Grouse Mountain, to Joseph Knott for $900. Knott and his sons erected a five-stamp steel mill in 1870 and ran it for a brief time, crushing 550 tons in the first year. The next year, Knott crushed 75 tons of ore, making only $1,060. The mill was near the summit, and the scarcity of water proved an economic hardship. The company got into litigation and went bankrupt. The first mining ventures in the district could recover only free gold in the quartz-bearing ore near the surface.

But staking claims continued, and cabins, a hotel and a saloon were constructed by miners. The establishment of the branch office of the Douglas County recorder's office took place at Bohemia City in 1868. A crusher was smashed in heavy snow, ending mining operations in the Bohemia Mining District until the early 1890s, when the recovery of gold in the veins of complex sulfides became economically feasible.

The lack of rich quartz veins on Johnson's ledge prompted Bird Farrier to confront Bohemia Johnson about his claim. Farrier noticed that the rich specimens Johnson showed everyone were not of the same formation as his Mystery Mine. Farrier asked Johnson about the ore specimens and found less than $700 in gold. Johnson told Farrier that the specimens were not from his current mine but from his other mine, located in a thick clump of brush. Johnson waved his hand, pointing across the gulch. He said he was working to sell the Mystery claim so that he could develop his other mine and then promised to take Farrier to it.

Johnson died before he could guide Farrier to the richer claim, thereby creating a mystery in more than name. Johnson told the other miners and prospectors in the area that his present Mystery claim "must have been a pocket."

The ownership of Johnson's claim passed on to the Musick Mining and Milling Company. The ore from the Musick Mine is darker in color, due to both a lower gold content and a greater lead sulfide and galena content than ore in the other producing mines in the district. That ore is lighter, as noted by Bird Farrier, due to more zinc and calcite content.

In 1890, Henry Pearson and Dr. W.W. Oglesby staked out the Annie claim, which yielded $26,000 over the next two years, reviving interest in the district. James A. Musick, while getting a drink of water in a mountain stream, found more gold in 1892. Like Bohemia Johnson twenty-nine years before, he found glittering gold shining up at him from a creek bed. Musick staked out two claims, the Los Angeles and the Defiance, and these became the Champion Mine, the richest mine in the Bohemia Mining District. It is only one mile east of Johnson's original claim. In 1905, the Oregon Securities Company bought the mine and began producing ore assaying at $29,000 per ton. Is the Champion Mine the site of Johnson's richer claim, the prospect that he pointed out to Bird Farrier?

A greenhorn prospector and photographer, Charles B. Bruneau, made a later gold discovery. From Cottage Grove, Bruneau showed up at the bunkhouse door one night in 1896 in his new miner's clothes announcing he had come to find gold. The experienced miners were sympathetic, and after fixing him dinner, they gave him directions to a good place to dig, two miles east of the old Mystery claim. The hardened miners laughed and joked about beginner's luck resulting in Bruneau hitting pay dirt in a spot they had ignored because it showed only specks of gold.

The next morning, Bruneau started digging at the spot where the old Knott Road intersected a stream. After three days, his ditch became wider and deeper, and the gold became richer. He staked his first claim when assay reports showed $12 per ton. Later, Bruneau staked five more claims and divided them into Helena Numbers 1 and 2. In addition, three years later, he struck the mother lode, where assay reports showed $3,000 a ton with selected samples showing an incredible $35,000 per ton.

In 1900, J.W. Harms made a new strike on Adams Mountain, three miles northwest of the main Musick Mines. The vein is five feet wide and shows

Musick Mine, Bohemian District. *Oregon Historical Society No. 6005764.*

Vesuvius Mine, Bohemian Mining District. This is in the area of Bohemia Johnson's Mystery Mine. *Oregon Historical Society picture No. 009178.*

free gold. In 1902, the Vesuvius claim, originally found by Swiss immigrants, began producing ore assaying at $29,000 a ton. The Ophir Mine has produced not one ounce of gold, but it is rich in silver and copper.

Considering all this information, either the Mystery Mine is the Champion Mine, or the two Helena Mines are the site of Johnson's Mystery Mine. Or it may be at Adams Mountain, if Bohemia Johnson's hand-waving gesture to Bird Farrier is correct. A U.S. Geological Survey made after World War II described the Bohemia District as having more potential than any other area in the Oregon Cascades, with over $10 million mined and twice that amount remaining in the rugged mountain terrain.

There is a chance that the richer gold claim lies elsewhere and remains undiscovered in the five-and-a-half-mile length and one-and-a-half-mile width of the main mineralization. By 1900, over two thousand claims in the Bohemia Mining district existed. Maybe Bohemian Johnson told the truth that his Mystery Mine was just another pocket that petered out.

White Cliffs of Gold

During the Indian Uprising of 1856, an elder Native American, Old Tenas Man, who had raven-black hair, eluded Rogue Indians by traveling up the headwaters of Myrtle Creek to a sheltered dry gulch to hide from his pursuers under towering cliffs of white rocks. Here he prepared for the coming winter by making a bark shelter and setting snares to catch food as well as trap those trying to catch him. Meanwhile, soldiers put down the uprising and placed the captured Rogue Indians on a reservation.

Pursuit of Old Tenas Man occurred because he was a trusted friend of white pioneers along the South Umpqua River, always warning settlers in advance of raids. In return, the settlers often lent Old Tenas Man a horse, traps, blankets and a rifle to hunt game. Local chiefs swore revenge on this ally of homesteaders and hoped to track him down and torture him. But the physically fit Native American eluded all trackers.

The next spring, Old Tenas Man appeared at the ranch of his friend Andrew Thomas, located twenty miles east of the old Eugene–Jacksonville stage line and just west of Coffee Creek, which flows south into the South Umpqua River. Here he found Thomas working in his blacksmith shop.

"You like much gold?" Old Tenas Man asked.

Old Tenas Man told how he had spent the winter in a bark hogan under towering white cliffs. The snow became so deep that he was kept there until

Sketch of Old Tenas Man. Oregonian, *July 27, 1948, page 77.*

it melted. When spring finally came, he crossed the formerly dry gulch now running with water from the melting snow.

"Gold, gold all over the place," said Old Tenas Man. "In bottom of creek that is dry in summer."

Then he poured over $400 worth of coarse nuggets on the top of Thomas's anvil.

"You say there's a lot more?" asked the startled Thomas.

"I saw gold all over the creek bed. After snow all in one moon, I will take you there. We will get much gold."

Old Tenas Man left the Thomas place for the settlement of Myrtle Creek, but before the month was up, a white man named Williams killed him. Settlers from miles around hunted for Williams to bring him to justice for killing their trusted friend. When they found Williams in a mountain cabin, he was dying from a strange disease. The Native American medico with the settlers explained that the spirit of Old Tenas Men had put a curse on the evil white men. They all decided not to hang Williams that day, allowing Ekone, the good spirit of Old Tenas Man, do its work.

After the snow melted, Thomas began what was to become a lifelong search for Tenas Man's gold. Later, his son resumed the search, but neither of them found any gold. It is strange that Andrew found no gold, because there is gold in the area. They were incompetent prospectors. The tributaries of North Myrtle Creek, Lee Creek and Buck Fork had placer production of

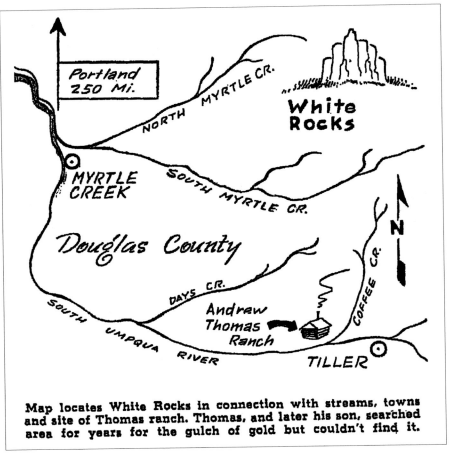

Map locates White Rocks in connection with streams, towns and site of Thomas ranch. Thomas, and later his son, searched area for years for the gulch of gold but couldn't find it.

White Rocks treasure map and sketch of Old Tenas Man. Oregonian, *June 27, 1948, page 77.*

$150,000 up to the year 1898. The bulk of the area where mineralization occurs is what is called metagabbro. These rocks have a texture like granite, having a mineral composition of plagioclase feldspar and lime-soda pyroxene altered to hornblende or chlorite. The feldspar is partly altered to an aggregate of quartz, muscovite, epidote and kaolin. Most gold nuggets found in North Myrtle Creek show little rounding and are attached to pieces of quartz both in the stream valleys and on hill slopes in decomposed rocks.

The Continental and Chieftain Mines on the north side of South Myrtle Creek are less likely sources of Old Tenas Man's placer gold, because no free gold is visible in the ores of these two mines and there are no recorded placer deposits on the South Fork. These placers, if near the site of Old Tenas Man's discovery, are not the source of the gold, because water flows in these named streams all year long, even in summer. The site of Old Tenas Man's gold, based on past placer production, is inside the watershed of North Myrtle Creek, in the shadows of White Rock (elevation 4,019 feet).

Laurel Hill Gold

Laurel Hill lies between Camp Creek and the Zigzag River, six miles east of Rhododendron, Oregon, on Highway 26. The area is the site of a cache buried during the last part of the 1800s by a highwayman who killed his partner and buried the gold along with his accomplice. Also, the area has over seventy-five mineral claims dating from 1927, and these prospect holes are still evident on the hill.

The robber then marked the burial site by a blaze on a cedar tree, but he never had a chance to recover the loot. He confessed his crime to his son on his deathbed and gave him directions for hunting the cache. The son found the blazed cedar tree and spent summers trying to recover the treasure. The cedar tree, a marker to the treasure site, has since fallen. But its location was no help to the son in his four-year search for the cache, and as far as is known, this cache has not been found.

The "Blazed Cedar Cache" originated when L.F. Pridemore, the manager of the Government Camp Hotel, narrated the story to writers, who first published it two decades later in a collection of *Oregon Curiosities* in 1939. Pridemore said the blazed cedar tree was visible around 1915 or later from his hotel on the top of Laurel Hill, where he had seen searchers looking for something.

Four roads traverse Laurel Hill: the one-way westbound road, the two-way Territorial Stage Road, the original 1925 Mount Hood Loop Highway and the current US Highway 26, constructed as a two-lane road and later widened and realigned as the present four-lane highway.

The stage robbery took place on the Territorial Stage Road, which became a two-way road completed in 1886 by blasting out a road around Laurel Hill. In the 1880s, the first tourists headed east from the Willamette Valley for vacation sites around Mount Hood. The first automobile traversed the road to Government Camp in 1903.

Ernest P. Sievers sunk a prospect hole ten feet square and twenty feet deep in the middle of the old Barlow Road one half mile from the old

Mount Hood Loop Road below the steep slope of Laurel Hill. Four assay reports confirmed mineralization up to 1.3 ounces of platinum, 0.1 ounce of gold, 4.3 ounces of uranium, 8.3 ounces of tin and 1.0 ounce of palladium. Sievers's statement appeared in the *Oregonian*: "I have found outcroppings on the other side of the hill. I have though I was going to hit the limits of the vein, but I have not scratched them. It is more like an ore body than a vein. The deeper I go for the gold the more minerals show up."

Within a week of Sievers's statement the *Oregonian*, during July 1927, stated that twenty-four mining claims were staked by Portland Motorists, "possessing little knowledge of geology, but abundant faith in their luck." There

OLD OREGON TRAIL (BARLOW ROAD), IN CASCADES MOUNTAINS, NEAR SUMMIT HOUSE, IN 1916

Barlow Road near Summit House, 1919. History of the Oregon Country *by Harvey Scott, 1924, page 151, author's copy.*

has been no commercial mining production on or near Laurel Hill. All those holes are due to prospectors and not modern searchers.

The easiest way to search for the cache is to look at areas of erosion and landslides where, hopefully, the treasure becomes unearthed. Native rhododendrons, which the pioneers believed were laurels for which the hill is named, have grown and covered the hillside since the time of the robbery. It is difficult to find clear areas where a metal-detector operator can get close to the ground, because the forest is so dense with Douglas firs and rhododendrons. Any clear areas are mostly solid rock and the products of landslides that cover acres of Laurel Hill. The cache could now be under a large fir or rhododendron grove.

The largest of the five chutes are not part of the Territorial Stage Road. They are a more famous and dangerous section of the old Barlow Road and the most western portion of the Oregon Trail dating from 1846 to 1866, when teamster wagon drivers lowered their wagons down the steep slopes by ropes or dragging trees as anchors. Therefore, each of the five rock chutes is outside the search area. Pioneers also cut down all the large trees near the chutes as drag logs, so no large cedars existed near the chutes at the time of the stage robbery.

Rhododendron grove, misnamed by pioneers as laurels, covering the search area of the Blazed Cedar Cache, showing how difficult it is to place a metal detector on the ground due to dense undergrowth. *Author's photo, 2009.*

Laurel Hill. This view shows the top of the chute of the Barlow Road, looking down and west. *Author's photo.*

Looking up (east) from the bottom of the chute on the Barlow Road section of the Oregon Trail. *Author's photo.*

Laurel Hill US Highway 26 marker, leading the way to the top of the chute of the original Barlow Road, constructed in 1845 to bypass the Columbia River Gorge. *Author's photo.*

GOVERNMENT CAMP HOTEL

Location on the south side of Mt. Hood. Headquarters for mountain climbers. Explore the nearby glaciers. Huckleberries will soon be ripe. Our hotel is famous for its huckleberry pies. For rates and reservations address

L. F. Prídemore

Proprietor Government Camp Hotel
RHODODERS, OR.
For Stage Phone E-155

Government Hotel advertisement. L.F. Pridemore, proprietor. Pridemore observed the treasure seeker at the base of the blazed cedar tree and told the story to a local newspaper reporter. Oregonian, *July 25, 1920, pagg 4.*

A major portion of the Laurel Hill section of the Stage Road lies just north of US Highway 26, crossing the highway where the Oregon Heritage Marker is today, located five feet beyond the eastbound shoulder. The Stage Road coincides east of the Tollgate Campground and a replica gate with the Bridle Path Trail, also labeled Forest Service Trail No. 795.

The robbery took place east, away from the western location of the old Toll House or Mountain House and the gates where wagon trains and stages regrouped at a log cabin to accommodate travelers and paid tolls on the Barlow Road. A holdup away from people near the summit of Laurel Hill is most plausible, because the stagecoach would have to slow down when descending Laurel Hill. This is my favorite area to search, because the blazed cedar was reported there by L.F. Pridemore of the Government Camp Hotel. One other area is just east of the Heritage Marker, beyond and away from the topside of the chutes.

In summary, a search with a metal detector, not available to the robber's son, centering east of Barlow Road Tollgate, which collected money until 1917 on the Territorial Stage Road, might prove profitable.

THE CASCADE CABIN CACHE

Mr. Pickett, a fugitive from justice, arrived at The Dalles in the 1860s posing as a man who had traveled around the Pacific Northwest doing prospecting here and there. He was worried about the hundred pounds of gold on his packhorse and bought copies of the *Boise Statesman* to read about a recent robbery in Idaho.

The robbery occurred on the Boise City–Owyhee stage. The Wells Fargo Company was sending large shipments of money and gold bullion. There was a section in the stage road where it started to descend steeply as it entered the mouth of a canyon. It was here that the stage usually arrived at dusk. The stagecoach driver usually stopped there to rest the horses before entering the canyon. Pickett waited beside the road as the Concord Coach began its descent. He placed a mask over his face and drew his rifle. He stopped the stage, yelling: "Stick them up or I will drill you! Now, throw down that Wells Fargo box."

There were no passengers, so there was only the driver to contend with. The masked Pickett tied and bound the driver and broke open the strongbox with his miner's pick. He made off with the gold greenbacks and gold bullion. The next day was a scorcher in the canyon. The driver was delirious from heat and thirst. It was days before he could say what happened, giving the robber time to head west to Oregon.

Pickett read that his former partner, Higgins, was arrested for the crime. His first impulse was to return to Idaho to turn himself in to local authorities, but he could not go through with it. Instead, he traveled southwest to the Cascade Mountains and found an old trapper's cabin. He lived there as a recluse for a decade. He buried the stolen gold under a nearby three-foot tree stump.

Pickett returned to Boise City seven years after the robbery, and no one recognized him. Convicted of the heist, Higgins was serving an eight-year sentence in the state penitentiary. Pickett became sick and wrote a confession that included where he had buried the gold, giving directions from his cabin to the stump.

While writing his confession, Pickett overlooked including details to locate the cabin itself. Wells Fargo agents traveled to The Dalles and searched south for the cabin in the high Cascades, giving up after a three-week search. Higgins received a pardon after the letter became public. The lost cabin with its buried gold created a sensation in the papers. One treasure hunter claimed to have found a cabin twenty miles south of the town of Hood River, where the Mount Hood National Forest boundary is today. But he failed to find gold under any tree stump. Another searcher from The Dalles knew of a cabin in the mountains. He traveled to the exact spot and returned home with no gold.

In 1957, hunters found an old fallen-down cabin in a remote valley along the northern slope of Mount Hood. The hunters stayed in the cabin for three days while hunting deer. After returning home to The Dalles, the hunters heard the story of Pickett's cabin and buried gold. They returned to the area but failed to find the cabin after three days of searching.

There is an outlaw story associated with a cabin at Horse Thief Meadows, just east of Mount Hood. The area's name came about because a near-sighted man failed to keep his horses from others pasturing in the mountain meadow. In 1884, a Mr. Phillips appeared in Hood River and hired David Rose Cooper Sr. from the community of Mount Hood to guide him in search of a cabin used by men who had robbed a stagecoach near Walla Walla. The loot stolen in 1880 totaled $25,000.

Cooper had a camping place on the east slope of Mount Hood. Cooper Spur separates Eliot Glacier from Newton Clark Glacier. In 1886, the stolen loot was rumored to be at Horse Thief Meadows near a cabin one mile west of State Highway 35 on Forest Service Road S-229 near Robin Hood Forest Camp. The cabin was still standing in 1940, and the gold was still missing.

The Red Blanket Mine

During the spring of 1897, Ed Schieffelin returned to Oregon to prospect the tributaries of the South Umpqua River in Douglas County. Schieffelin had discovered the fabulous mines and town of Tombstone, Arizona, where naysayers had said "all he would find was his tombstone." He named the site Tombstone to show he had "fooled them all right. I found what I was after, silver, almost pure silver!" Along with two other mines, he found the Lucky Cuss and Tough Nut, selling all three for $1.5 million.

Schieffelin spent his younger years on a farm near Woodsville, Oregon, which is now the current town of Rogue River. Historian Hugh Bancroft described Schieffelin as "a man of large and powerful build, a type of the physically perfect man; his bronzed face and flowing hair and beard, and his clear blue eyes, tell of the free and open life of the plains and mountains."

Schieffelin stood six feet tall and weighed 175 pounds. He never wore a tie or top hat. Instead, when he dressed up, he wore a silk handkerchief tied around his neck and a Stetson. His only piece of jewelry was a gold timepiece. His boots were custom-made, constructed of fancy stitched calfskin. The boots came over the knees, making them rattlesnake-proof.

Schieffelin refurbished an existing old cabin on Moore Creek near the head of Days Creek, twenty miles east of Canyonville. He made this the center of his operations while prospecting the surrounding country. His mail and supplies arrived at the George Jackson homestead on the mouth of Days Creek. His camp tender, cook and driver, twenty-three-year-old Charles Warren, picked up the mail and supplies, earning twenty dollars a month and a stake in all the gold they found. In May 1897, Warren went to visit his family at Woodsville and intended to return to the Jackson homestead, when Schieffelin had planned to be at the cabin.

Alex Orme, a mutual friend of both men, often traveled to visit Schieffelin. Orme became concerned when Ed did not return for his supplies after several weeks. He hiked seven miles from the Jackson homestead up to Moore Creek and found Ed Schieffelin on the doorstep of his cabin, sprawled over the mortar on which he had been grinding a sample of ore.

He appeared dead from natural causes, possibly a heart attack, as there were no marks of violence on his body. An inquest came to the same conclusion. The acting coroner, Dr. W.H. DeVore, determined that Ed died of a heart attack on May 12, 1897.

The prospector, age forty-nine, had on his person $68.75 in coins and his $400 gold watch, ruling out robbery of the cabin. In the cabin was a half-filled bottle of whiskey, a pan of burnt beans on the cold stove and charred biscuits in the Dutch oven. Schieffelin had been dead

Ed Schieffelin, founder of Tombstone, Arizona, and his Red Blanket Mine. *Jacksonville, Oregon Museum photo, 1971, now Historical Jacksonville Inc.*

for more than a week. Justice of the Peace William Stock wrapped the body in a blue blanket and buried Schieffelin in a rough box, as reported in the *Ashland Tidings* of May 17, 1897. His brother Effingham believed that Ed died from the chemicals he used to make the mineral assay and not from a heart attack induced by alcohol and fatigue.

After the recording of Schieffelin's will in Washington County, Oregon, Ed's wish for a burial on a hill three miles west of Tombstone, Arizona, was fulfilled. His three brothers buried the body with his prospector clothes and tools beneath a marker twenty-five-feet high, such as prospectors build when locating a mining claim. His brothers and wife divided his estate of $75,000.

Schieffelin was rumored to have been found face-down next to a mortar and pestle inside the cabin. According to legend, the pestle contained grayish blue quartz flecked with beads of gold. In a jar nearby were more ore samples that assayed at $2,000 a ton in gold, along with tobacco tins containing samples of lesser value. In his diary, Ed's last entry read, "Struck her rich again, by God." An earlier entry read, "richer than Tombstone."

Charlie Warren, on hearing of Schieffelin's death, returned to the cabin and later added more details of the death scene. In 1895, when Schieffelin returned to Oregon, he bought two wool blankets, one blue and one red. On his overnight prospecting trips in Oregon, Ed often packed cooking utensils wrapped in a wool blanket. In the cabin, Warren saw the blue blanket and noticed that two cooking pots were missing. This led Warren to deduce that the gold ore was one night's travel from the cabin and that Schieffelin had left the pots to mark the site, hoping to return the next day.

Warren described old Ed this way: "His mind was set like a steel trap, and he would follow the plan of the night before. After retiring each night, he would plan what he intended to do the next day." This "bull-headed trait" made Ed a success where other miners had failed. Schieffelin was already rich. He wanted another strike to his credit like Tombstone and would search for nothing less, according to Charlie Warren.

Schieffelin had a sense of humor, a flair for showmanship and an appreciation for life's irony—such as the fact that he might have struck it rich again on the day he died.

The red blanket allegedly left behind at the gold discovery site led to the legend of the Lost Red Blanket Mine. Warren did not mention a Schieffelin diary or ledger left behind in the cabin in the narrative he gave just after Schieffelin's death. Warren failed to mention that Schieffelin owned a red blanket during the last eighteen months he, Warren, worked as a camp helper.

In another version of the Lost Red Blanket Mine, written by author Stewart Holbrook, there is no mention of the diary entry. In this version, the gold strike appeared in a letter mailed two weeks before Ed's death: "I have found stuff here in Oregon that will make Tombstone look like salt." Along with the letter, there was a vague map that no one could decipher, apparently giving directions to a new strike, which was passed on to Schieffelin's Canadian-born nephew. The nephew in turn passed it on to a comrade before dying during World War I at the Battle of Verdun. Holbrook later saw the map and letter, believing it to be genuine. The writing is beyond doubt that of Ed Schieffelin, because "I know this man and have seen the paper."

Which story is correct is uncertain. They both could be true, because the letter, map and diary disappeared, and the whole truth is unknown. Another version states that the contents of the letter to Ed's wife, Mary, says only that he found "a prospect at last," with no mention of its value. This lost letter is the only reference to a diary in a February 1900 letter from Mary to Frank M. Moore, who leased his cabin to Ed and continued the search after Ed's death.

Fred Minqua of Glendale, Oregon, staked it as the Tombstone Prospect, believing it might have been the Red Blanket Mine that writer Dale Vincent placed twenty miles south of Days Creek in the Canyon Creek drainage at Quines Creek in 1946. In 1984, Minqua found in a shallow discovery cut the beginnings of a shaft 10 feet deep, along with a rusted shovel and a pick with rotted-out handles at the 2,720-foot elevation. A road running through the mountain pass covered up the entire original prospect except for the dump on the north side of the road. Road construction exposed two small cuts 200 feet southwest of the old prospect site. Minqua had collected high-grade ore with pyrite and visible gold. But three of the iron-stained vein quartz samples never proved as rich as Minqua's original ore samples and were not like the blue quartz found in the Moore cabin.

The main difficulty in locating Schieffelin's last prospect is that the lost diary or map give no directions or distances from his cabin on Days Creek. Charlie Warren and others believed that Ed could have trekked up to twenty miles from his cabin on a day's travel and camped for the night.

Many searchers have prospected along Coffee Creek and dug prospect holes on the fifth stream to the east of Days Creek, where Ed panned gold as a kid. They hoped to find the lode vein, which is the source of placer gold in Texas Gulch.

There are reasons to believe the site of the gold prospect is located somewhere in the Coffee Creek drainage. Days Creek has never been a source of either placer or lode gold. Coffee Creek got its name in 1858 when a soldier, after a day of chasing hostile Native Americans, bitterly complained to his unit about the lack of coffee, even after finding gold in the creek. Schieffelin was always interested in returning to Coffee Creek, where he prospected in his youth.

Ed bought a blue-and-yellow-trimmed buggy and two white horses. The postal worker at Milo, Dan Perdue, told Ed that he could not take his big carriage and team up Coffee Creek. The easiest route would be up Days Creek to Moore Creek and hike over the ridge five miles to Texas and Thornton Gulches by the Brush Creek trail and then to Coffee Creek. Here, seven miles north on Days Creek, Ed rebuilt the old Moore cabin and found a formation of red quartz to the east toward Coffee Creek. After three weeks of searching, he found a place where the formation broke away to a ledge of blue quartz, which he brought back to his cabin, believing it was a prospect at least deserving of an assay. The cabin stood until the 1930s, when it fell into dangerous disrepair and was razed.

Less than three miles from upper Days Creek lay the South Myrtle Creek and Letitia Creek lode gold discovery sites, made sometime after Ed's death at the Chieftain and Continental Mines. They totaled more than $200,000 from 1898 to 1940. Mineralization at these two lode mines occurs in visible outcroppings of stringers of quartz and sulfides in the metagabbro rocks of the Western Cascades, which is more like the Schieffelin quartz sample than the cemented gravel beds of the Coffee Creek area.

At the Little Chieftain Mine in 1960, renamed the Nugget City Mine, a new quartz vein running north–south—as opposed to the old veins running east–west—assayed at $13.04 per ton. Its announcement proved that there was still gold-bearing quartz on Myrtle Creek. Ron Moore, president of the Heirloom Gold Company, based in the town of Myrtle Creek, Oregon, suggested that the area "has a wealth of minerals covered up by foliage and there's too much of it for our company or any one company to take care of."

Charles L. Schieffelin, Ed's brother, located gold ore fifteen miles from the eastern side of Days Creek. Charles staked a quartz claim bearing gold, silver and lead on September 15, 1900. He named it Last Prospect. The ore was not rich and so was not the rich strike made by his brother. The Coffee Creek Placers originate in the ancient, cemented gravel beds and could not come from blue-gray quartz found at the cabin at the time of Schieffelin's death.

There is a Red Blanket Creek in Jackson County. It flows into the Middle Fork of the Rogue River south of Prospect. One writer, Ruby El Hult, who never knew the exact location of the mining cabin on Moore Creek, suggested that Red Blanket Creek could be the Schieffelin prospect. However, the name came about when pioneer settlers traded red blankets for fertile Indigenous land in the area and has nothing to do with the Red Blanket legend. The likely explanation is Ed Schieffelin's claim, that he found a small gold and silver prospect near South Myrtle Creek three miles or more due west of his Moore Creek cabin. The last ore sample Ed had assayed was worth only seven dollars a ton. His brothers discovered this in the cabin.

Seventy-three-year-old Charlie Warren said in 1946 of Schieffelin's and his lost prospect, "Whoever finds the red wool blanket will find that lost gold mine, and it will be rich, or Ed wouldn't have been interested in it."

The fabulous riches alluded to in the lost diary and letter and embellished by later writers over the years have become the extravagant claim of another legend of a lost bonanza in the American West.

EASTERN OREGON

Gold Dredge Nuggets

Baker County and other mining areas of the Pacific Northwest had dredges to recover gold from streams. One of these areas was in Washington State, west of the small town of Liberty, where US Highway 97 parallels Swauk Creek in Kittitas County. In the decades of the nineteenth-century mining boom, Swauk Creek, a tributary to the Yakima River, yielded tons of placer gold. In the twentieth century, a large California mining company imported a gold dredge to extract the remaining gold left behind by early prospectors.

The dredge turned the entire streambed upside down above the bedrock and left behind ugly windrows of coarse gravel and boulders along its course. The dredges have a rotating screen that sifts out sand and fine gravel and discards all large material, including large gold nuggets.

One day in 1941, visitors were watching the Swauk Creek dredging operation when a woman picked up a curious yellow rock weighing about a pound and a half. "Look what I found," she cried out to her companions. "What do you think it is?"

The yellow stone proved to be a large gold nugget worth more than $400 at the current price of gold of $35 an ounce. Since the time of the first discovery, other gold nuggets exist among those enormous boulder piles and mining debris, including a giant two-pound nugget found by Nathan Goodheart.

The reason these nuggets remain behind is that they were too large to pass through the rotating screen on the mining dredge so exist now along with all the remaining dredge spoils. Swauk Creek, it seems, contained dozens of gold nuggets larger than three-quarters of an inch in diameter. The larger nuggets remain in the dredging spoils of Swauk Creek and other old mining areas of the West like Baker County.

The Sumpter Valley Dredge State Park, twenty-five miles west of Baker City, is a good place to search for remaining gold nuggets among the piles of gravel of the dredge spoils along the Powder River. This site offers a historical museum, an old mining dredge and a restored narrow-gauge railroad that offers rides. The area has become a prime bird and wildlife habitat.

The Miners Jubilee at Baker City, held during the third week of July, celebrates the mining history of Baker County. The celebration offers additional attractions, including a two-day rodeo, gold-panning contests and more.

Baker County, named for Oregon senator Edward Baker, who died during the first year of the American Civil War, is one of the best areas in Oregon to look for lost prospects and gold. There are lively ghost towns in the area, including Sumpter, Granite and Bourne. They provide a good starting place to prospect for valuable ores.

THE LOST CAVALRYMEN MINE

On June 3, 1878, General O.O. Howard summoned two companies of the U.S. Army consisting of eighty men to Fort Boise as reinforcements during the height of the Bannock Indian War, where they were under the command of Captain Reuben F. Bernard. Navigating by compass from Fort Harney, heading due east at a latitude of 43°40", the cavalrymen arrived at the mouth of the Boise River at the Snake River five days later.

Captain Jonathan Keeney, formerly of Missouri, and sons Peter and James talked to three soldiers, who told them they had found a rich gold deposit. The three soldiers showed Captain Keeney, who owned the Boise River Ferry, ore samples heavily laden with gold. The soldiers also told Keeney that they marked the spot of the prospect well near their night camp, three days' journey southwest from the Fort Boise Ferry, known at the time as the Riverside Ferry.

The three soldiers hoped to return as soon as possible after conquering the Native Americans and file a mining claim on their newly discovered riches. Jon Keeney never saw the men again and wondered if they were among the five soldiers killed at Battle Creek in Southwestern Idaho. Months later, Keeney went west to find the mine of the three cavalrymen.

After searching for weeks, he did find one of the camps three days' ride from the horse-powered ferry he had purchased.

Keeney spent months looking for the bonanza, giving his name to Keeney Ridge and Keeney Creek in the process. The Keeney family sold the ferry five months later to Sam McDowell. He renamed it McDowell's Ferry.

On March 17, 1951, the *Oregon Journal* published a map showing the cavalrymen's camp of 1878 on an unnamed northern tributary of Dry Creek. The map and article about the Lost Sheepherder Mine brought dozens of searchers during March and April 1951. The camp, according to the *Oregon Journal* map, is located more than seventy-three airline miles from Fort Harney, which is more than a day's ride by horse from Fort Harney. The suggested area of search was an idealized location, thirty miles south of Vale and hemmed in by the northern landmarks Freezeout Mountain, Sourdough Mountain and Grassy Mountain. To the east were Oxbow Basin and Dry Creek Butte, with a portion of Dry Creek to the south.

Among the searchers in this area were a premedical student, Bert D. Campbell Jr., age twenty-four, and Judge Sewell Stanton. They searched the area for years for the mine, which they believed to be the same lost prospect

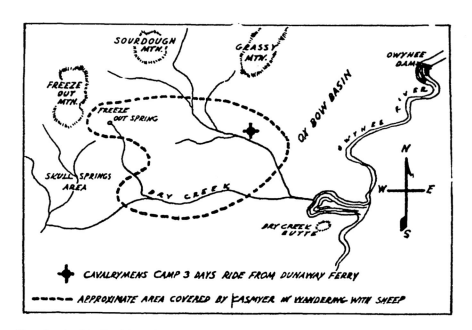

Sheepherder Idealized Search Area. Oregonian, *March 11, 1951.*

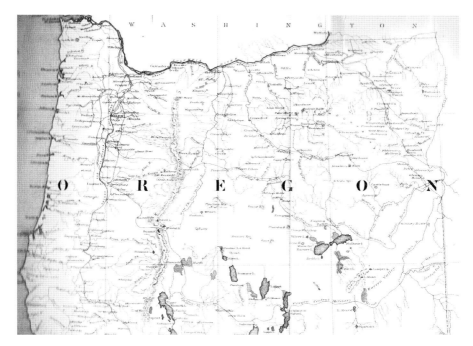

Oregon, 1888. *Hubert Bancroft,* History of Oregon, *Volume 1, 1888, author's copy.*

as the Lost Sheepherder Mine of Victor Casmyer in Malheur County. The belief that the Cavalrymen Mine and the Lost Sheepherder Mine are the same mine is an error. A one-day ride by horse east of Fort Harney would not be seventy-three miles but closer to twenty miles, where the main area of search starts for the gold of the cavalrymen.

THE LOST SHEEPHERDER MINE

Victor E. Casmyer was a husky, blond sheepherder who was dying of spotted fever in 1912. He was working for two Basque sheep men in a camp thirty miles south of Vale. His condition became grave, and the concerned camp cook, Peter Rameau, decided to put Casmyer on a packhorse and take him into Vale, where he slept in a livery stable owned by Billy Huffman.

When Huffman saw how sick Casmyer had become, he talked the young sheepherder into renting a room at the local hotel, where Casmyer would be more comfortable and away from the cold. Huffman became a fast friend, looked in on the sick man every day and brought him food and drink whenever he asked. During Huffman's last visit before Casmyer died, Casmyer raved about a gold prospect he had discovered in the Owyhee desert.

"Billy, there is enough gold there to make all my friends and relatives rich. The vein is eighteen inches thick."

Huffman believed that Casmyer was delirious from fever, so when the herder told him where the gold strike was located and offered to draw a map to show him the way to it, Huffman tried to sooth him, saying, "When you're well, we'll both go out together and stake a claim."

"I know I'm dying," said Casmyer. "I will never live long enough to go there. I want you to find it. Look in my bedroll left in the stable, and you will find ore samples there. Once you see them, you will believe me."

The next morning, Huffman unrolled Casmyer's bedroll. As Casmyer claimed, the ore samples fell on the stable's earth floor with a thud. They were mostly gold. Huffman hurried over to the hotel, only to discover at the front desk that Casmyer died sometime in the night or early morning from spotted fever. The ore assayed between $10,000 to $30,000 per ton.

Huffman had lost his chance to learn the mine's location. He told other townsfolk about the eighteen-inch vein of gold in the desert and his lost opportunity to be rich. Local old-timers remembered the story as almost identical to another local legend: the Lost Gold of the Cavalrymen. Dozens of searchers went out to look at all the water holes and camps that Casmyer might have used in the Dry Creek drainage, from Freezeout Mountain east to the Owyhee River, where they discovered fossils, agates, semiprecious gems and petrified wood, but no gold.

In April 1958, L.L. Mills of Kelso, Washington, went out to search for the Blue Bucket Placer. According to the diary of Jessie Harritt and historian Captain O.C. Applegate, Mills believed that the Steve Meek caravan had traveled south along the South Fork of the Malheur River, not the North Fork, as believed. Mills and son-in-law C.L. Carlson prospected around Chalk Butte, Coyote Wells at the head of Dry Creek and south to Skull Springs and Steen Mountain. Like everyone else, they found no gold in the area. The gold may lie ten miles to the west of Freezeout Mountain, centering on Crowley Road, north of Quartz Butte, where quartz is a gangue rock surrounding gold. Searchers looking more than thirty miles south of Vale near the last known camp of Victor Casmyer overlooked the main search area for the two mines.

The Owyhee Gold Cache

The Owyhee Breaks of Southeastern Oregon, bordering the western shore of Lake Owyhee, contain a cave holding the remains of twelve soldiers killed by Bannock Indians, as well as a rumored payroll of two saddlebags of gold coins. The doomed U.S. Cavalry unit traveled from Fort Yellowstone, Wyoming, to deliver a payroll to the paymaster at Fort Bidwell, California, sometime after 1866, when the camp was established and before the outbreak of the Bannock Indian War of 1878.

A surprise daylight attack caught the soldiers in their bedrolls. Native Americans flashed their knives. It ended when shots at the army patrol rang out. The Bannock warriors feared acts of reprisal from the U.S. Army after signing a peace treaty in 1867 and hauled the soldiers' bodies and equipment into the cave to eliminate the evidence. The Bannocks had signed the treaty ending their earlier part in the Snake Indian War. The treaty created two reservations and access to traditional camas gathering areas.

The last Native American guardian of the cave, "Modoc Annie," was born in 1904 on Mule Creek near Drewsey in northern Malheur County. She favored the name Modoc. She described the cave after seeing it for the first time when her father, Fred L. Gregg, illuminated the cave using sagebrush torches. Skulls with "hollow eyes" topped the bodies of the soldiers, guarded by rifles stacked like "little teepees."

Modoc "tended" the cave with her trapper father but never again entered it after his death. Modoc's father, part Scotsman and part Cherokee, heard about the cave from local Paiute Indians before locating the cache in 1884, the same year he migrated from the Oklahoma Indian Territory. Modoc's mother, Betty Schation, was a second cousin of a warrior of the band of Captain Jack, who battled the U.S. Army at the Lava Beds in Northern California during the 1873 Modoc Indian War.

After her first marriage, Modoc started work as a buckeroo at the age of seventeen in Eastern Oregon and went by the name Anne Day, or "Indian Annie." She later married Robert Thomas, a cotton gin worker, described as a "powerful, quiet man" who believed absolutely in her story.

Lloyd Russell, part owner and main promoter of the Lake Owyhee Resort, believed Modoc's story and brought her and her husband from Huron, California, and offered Modoc a $500 reward if she could find the soldiers' cave. Modoc feared flying and refused to take an airplane to the Pinnacle airstrip at Hole-in-the-Ground or to Morrison Ranch near Birch Creek.

Top: Owyhee Lake. Arthur W. Redman is shown in boat, 1966. *Author's photo.*

Bottom: A.W. Redman exploring the western shore of Owyhee Lake, circa 1966. *Author's photo.*

Opposite: P Ranch Barn, Frenchglen, Oregon. *Author's photo.*

Instead, the search party of fourteen people had to travel overland, departing Ontario, Oregon, at 4:00 a.m. on April 1, 1959, in a grueling thirty-five-mile drive south by jeep on a dirt road to the backed-up waters of the Owyhee Reservoir. The expedition included three drivers from the town of Vale: Bill Swift, George Van Horn and Hilton Clark. Also on the trek were *Oregon Journal* writer Tom McAllister, television adventure host Bob Brown, Al Seibel and Elton Howard from Hermiston, Lloyd Russell, Bill Mynatt and his wife from Grants Pass and Merle Doane and Don Grafe from Ontario, Oregon.

Twelve hours later, the expedition stopped under the towering cliffs of the Hole-in-the-Ground Ranch. A thunderstorm the night before had turned the road to slick mud with the consistency of gumbo. The party slowed at one point to a one-mile-per-hour crawl, taking four hours to climb up a one-thousand-foot grade on the road to the Owyhee River. "You fellows couldn't drive an old woman with a whip," complained Annie.

At the end of the eight-mile journey, Modoc hobbled to a slide of broken basalt beside the Owyhee River, her left arm immobilized and one leg sore from being in a car wreck the night before. She looked at the red bluffs, compared the area to a little Grand Canyon and promptly judged the approach to be wrong. Modoc Annie was a publicity stunt by Lloyd Russell to promote his resort on Lake Owyhee. The article printed in the *Oregonian* begins on April Fool's Day. The party drove back to Ontario, arriving there at 1:00 a.m.

But five members considered the legend true or at least worth considering and formed a second expedition led by William Swift of Vale. The Swift Party started out on April 3 with camping equipment and a determination for an extended search to find the cave or disprove the legend. There is no record in the *Oregon Journal* of their search for the cave.

Modoc Annie was correct in asserting that the path to the Owyhee Gold Cache was not opposite Birch Creek on the road to the historic Hole-in-the-

Ground Ranch. There are three other western approaches to the canyon lands of the Owyhee Breaks within twenty-five miles of one another.

Located to the northernmost part is Red Butte Canyon, then Dead Man Gulch, Three Finger Gulch and Dry Creek. One of these four could be the correct approach leading to the Owyhee Soldier Cave.

Vanorman Cache

Alexis Vanorman left Fort Hall, Idaho Territory, to lead a group of eight wagons consisting of forty-eight people in August 1860 under a six-man military escort. The fifty-four travelers were following the Oregon Trail west to the Willamette Valley in Oregon. The military unit left the wagon train, leaving only three soldiers to serve as guards, as the unit had experienced no encounters with Native tribes.

Two weeks later, a band of Snake Indians attacked the Vanorman-led party just south of present-day Adrian near the Snake River, killing nineteen. The survivors abandoned their wagons on the evening of September 10, 1860, fleeing by horseback and on foot. Vanorman and others made their way to the Snake River. They headed north to the Owyhee River, where they set up camp on the eastern side two miles south of the river's mouth, in the shadow of a fifty-foot butte. There they awaited a rescue party.

The bodies of Vanorman and five others of the party, all filled with arrows, were found by soldiers north of the Burnt River. A military relief column on October 17, 1866, led by Captain Fred T. Dent, the brother-in-law of General U.S. Grant, rescued the remainder of the party.

Mary Myers, who settled at Medford, received Vanorman's belongings. She never talked about the Vanorman-led party because of evidence of cannibalism among the few survivors occurring on October 7.

The party camped on the Owyhee were growing too weak to stand, let alone walk. They ate grass, weeds and sagebrush. Five dead remained unburied because the survivors lacked the strength to dig graves. It was twenty-five days since they had left the wagons behind in Idaho. On the morning of October 7, a prayer and a vote by all adult members took place. The vote, about whether to eat some of their own, followed heated discussion. The vote was unanimous. An old kettle was filled with water, and Mrs. Chase's children's remains served as food for the entire party.

Months later, among Vanorman's possessions, a letter by Mrs. Myers was found. It described the events that had occurred and what happened to the

Owyhee River Canyon, looking west, near the location of the Vanorman cache. *Author's photo.*

strongbox containing $5,000 in gold coins entrusted to him by his brother Wilhelm for the purchase of land and supplies in Oregon. Vanorman had gathered all the gold he could during the attack of September 10.

The ravaged survivors carried the heavy box to the Owyhee River camp. Vanorman took the chest across the Owyhee River and buried it on the west side of the river. He etched his initials, A.V., deeply into a large tock that came to a point. This served as a landmark; he buried the money next to it. Few treasure seekers have sought this cache, as it is not as well-known as others in Eastern Oregon.

LOST OWYHEE CANNON

During the Indian campaigns of the Snake Indian War, Major L.H. Marshall led an eighty-five-man expedition on May 11, 1866, from Fort Boise, Idaho, to scout the headwaters of the Bannock tribe in Southeastern Oregon. He found a large force of Bannocks at Three Forks on June 1, between the South and Middle Forks. The river was impassible at that point, and Marshall decided to move downriver eight miles, where he crossed with his men by constructing a makeshift raft.

As they advanced up the bluff, Native American warriors concealed behind rocks fired on them. A battle commenced that lasted over four hours. Seven Indians were killed and twelve wounded. The three hundred estimated Bannocks were secure in their position behind the rocks. The U.S. Army lost one man, a Private Phillips. He was killed, scalped and dragged up a cliff by a rope around his neck. Lieutenant Silas Pepoon wished to rescue Phillips but was forbidden by Major Marshall, who decided to give up and withdraw across the river.

Marshall, along with eighty men, retreated across the Owyhee River in the only vessel the U.S. Army had there. It overturned, and the howitzer, provisions and ammunition were lost. Major Marshall left four men on the opposite side of the Owyhee. They were cut off after the swamping of the flimsy raft.

According to historian Hugh Bancroft and the Idaho Historical Society, the cannon has not been found, and it remains to this day at the bottom of the Owyhee River, about eight miles downriver from Three Forks in extreme Southeastern Oregon, twelve miles to the west of the Idaho border and above the Half Mile Rapids. If recovered, the cannon would be a valuable artifact of Pacific Northwest military history.

5

CENTRAL OREGON

The Skeleton Rock Cache

John Holt and his partner, Jack, held up a stagecoach in 1870 four miles south of Prineville carrying a U.S. Army payroll and a strongbox with $50,000 in gold. Jack killed the guard. The pair headed toward Sanford Creek, which flowed into the Crooked River valley. There, a band of Native American warriors started chasing them.

The twosome was able to stay ahead of the Indigenous people by remaining in the brush and willows of the creek until they reached the Crooked River, where their situation became dire. They saw a large hill capped by rocks and decided to climb to the top and fend off the attack. They ditched their horses, grabbed the mail sacks and strongbox and scurried up the hill.

Shots rang out, hitting both men. The wounded robbers were just able to make it to the top of the rocks and ward off the attack. Jack soon died from his wounds. Holt, who suffered a leg wound, was able to hide Jack's body among the mail sacks and strongbox before sneaking off the rock in the dark of night and move toward the willows alongside Crooked River. Holt then followed the river downstream to Prineville.

Unfortunately for Holt, an army patrol was in Prineville, and they had heard about a wounded man arriving in Prineville. They informed local authorities, who arrested him for stage robbery. Holt was released from prison at age seventy in 1923.

To find his old cache, Holt returned to Prineville and hired a young man in August 1925 to guide him to the rock where he hid the treasure. Holt tried to describe the area to his guide, but after days of searching, they gave up. After leaving Prineville, the guide described the search to two local ranchers, Elton and Wayne Carey.

They gave the rock its name when they found a skeleton in one of the crevices on top of the rock. The rock was half filled with sand and covered with rye grass, human teeth, a rib and arm bones. They also found pieces of rotting wood and scraps from horseshoes that may have served as reinforcement to a strongbox, but they found no bones from the lower part of the skeleton.

Since 1983, the rock has been the site of geo-caching. This strongbox is hidden among the rocks along the south side of the Prineville Reservoir, sixteen miles south of Prineville, where the reservoir backs up against the rock.

Searchers should use a boat, raft or kayak to reach the rock, because the south side of Skeleton Rock has no roads leading to the search area and going there on foot would involve a long trek. But when you reach the rock, the back side from the south has a gentler slope to the top. The gold, along with the lower part of the skeleton, is there waiting for a diligent searcher.

THE LOST COWPOKE MINE

In the northern part of Lake County, south of the Lost Forest, a cattle driver saw a large black rock that raised his curiosity. He chipped off a piece of the rock. He later forgot about it for the most part, remembering only the rock's heavy weight. Another story claims it was a sheepherder who found the black rock somewhere in Lake County.

When the cowpoke or sheepherder rediscovered the piece of rock in his pocket, he remembered that his Lakeview dentist, Dr. C.P. Mason, had mineralogy as a hobby, so he decided to show the rock to Mason. One month later, Dr. Mason called the man to his office to tell him that the piece of black rock assayed over $5,000 to the ton. The problem now was that the man could not remember where he came across the ore sample, only that it was somewhere in the northern section of Lake County.

Later, in March 1925, prospectors Taylor and Picklesimer discovered a ledge of ore near Paisley. Newspaper reports revived interest in the cowpoke's gold and the Blue Bucket Placer. Could Paisley be the site of this placer? Since Paisley is in the central part of Lake County and the Paisley prospect later proved to have no commercial value, having no gold nuggets or assays close to $5,000 a ton, the search for the Cowpoke's Mine and Blue Bucket took place elsewhere, away from the Paisley site.

No Paisley gold frenzy appears in the Portland newspapers or in the Oregon Department of Geology and Mineral Industries 1968 publication *Gold and Silver in Oregon.* Prospecting occurred for lead, zinc and cinnabar, and claims staked for these ores exist, but there are none for gold in the area before 1968.

Various parts of the cowpoke's story have circulated among historians of Southeastern Oregon for years. Hal H. Ogle of Klamath Falls heard a garbled version of the story, which he repeated to writer Ruby El Hult. Ogle believed that Dr. Bernard Daly, who is also a judge, was the individual who received the gold sample from the cowpoke. When Judge Daly died on January 6, 1920, he left a provision in his will leaving the gold and assay report to the cowpoke.

Leslie Shaw of the *Lake County Examiner* checked Daly's will and found nothing related to misplaced gold. But according to the newspapers, Daly left $800,000 for an education fund for Lake County students.

The main piece of information Ogle added to this legend was that the cowboys' rendezvous point was at Sand Springs, on the southern edge of the Lost Forest, after they became lost during a cattle drive. Ms. Hult erroneously placed the cowpoke's forgotten gold in the Lost Forest, and this was repeated by other writers.

J.A. Gordon, president of the First National Bank of Klamath Falls, related another story of misplaced or lost gold similar to the cattle driver's tale. Around 1970, a man came into this bank with a small bottle of light-colored sand. When asked by Gordon what was inside the bottle, the unnamed man replied, "gold," and asked for an assay. "In a day's walk from here, I can arrive at a place where I can get some more."

The state government assay found the bottle of sand to be almost 85 percent gold. The Oregon Department of Geology and Mineral Industries tried to locate the man but failed to do so. If the report is true, an unknown gold source is located only fifteen to twenty miles from Klamath Falls.

The Lost Forest is a relic pine forest dating from the last ice age—a unique fourteen-square-mile oasis of juniper and ponderosa pine located fifty miles northeast of Christmas Lake in an area where ponderosa pine does not survive in a landscape with so little rainfall. The unique subterrain of sandy soil allows the pine to tap subsurface water to survive.

In the Lost Forest, there are no ledges of black rock atop the sandy soil. I toured the forest and did not observe surface black rocks of mineralogical interest. In addition, this forest is not a place where cowboys can find and drive cattle. The only knowledge about the lost cattle driver's gold is that it is located south of the Lost Forest in Lake County, not at Sand Springs, where the cowboys searched, nor to the north of the thoroughly prospected area of the Paisley gold hunt. The narratives of Hal Ogle are partly true, and the location somewhere in the northern part of Lake County is questionable.

Modern-day cattle drive, Deschutes County, Oregon. *Author's photo.*

One other site in Lake County to search is the High-Grade District, fifteen miles south of Lakeview. It is six miles east of New Pine Creek on the Oregon border south into Modoc County, California, along the crest of the Warner Mountains. There are seven gold mines in the district, all in California, known as the Hoag District until 1912.

The Modoc Mine, which dates from 1905, when a sheepherder found a little gold in the area, is the northernmost mine in the district. It is less than one mile south of the Oregon border at 7,549 feet. The district stretches north to Crane Mountain, where quartz and gold occurs north to Drake's Peak.

The cowpoke's or sheepherder's gold might lie in the small mineral-bearing veins in the High-Grade District. The gold would exist only along epithermal veins of replacement or tertiary rhyolite that underlies basalt, where thunder eggs and agates exist. No production records for the Oregon section of the district exist. This could be an overlooked area to prospect, along surface fractures of yellow rhyolite, where manganese, stained material and quartz exist. This may be the source of the mineral the cattle driver or sheepherder left in the care of C.P. Mason of Lakeview.

LOST CRYSTAL CAVE

In the fall of 1896, Newt Cobb and other sheepherders, herding sheep for shearing, accidentally discovered the opening of a cave one day's ride by horse southeast of Millican near Pine Mountain. The sheepherders saw an approaching morning storm and decided to stop and brew cups of coffee. While looking for dry sagebrush and juniper branches to start a fire, one of them almost fell into a small opening in the ground.

They believed they had found another lava cave, which is typical in Lake County. After constructing torches, they squeezed into the cave and found a room with walls and ceilings covered with jewels that radiated light from the flickering torches. They broke off some of the stunning samples and rode back to the Millican Ranch.

Seven years later, Nick Paul Smith, the owner of a Bend hardware store on Wall Street, saw the crystals. This piqued his interest, as he was fascinated by rocks and minerals. Smith decided to go out before the onset of winter in 1904 to search for the Crystal Cave. Somehow, he found the cave late in the afternoon of the third day of his search. He went into the cave, broke off four crystals and determined that the cave contained $1 million of calcite crystals.

An early winter storm was approaching, so he hurried back to Bend. Later, he gave two crystals to a fellow mineralogist. She was a nonrelative known as "Aunt" Moll Nichols. Molly kept the crystals for her mineral collection at her home in Tumalo, Oregon, showing them to local rockhounds until her death in 1938 at the age of ninety.

Spring arrived late in the Oregon High Desert that year. When it finally came, the snow disappeared, along with all traces of Smith's path. The entire area appeared unfamiliar to him. For years thereafter, Smith searched for the Crystal Cave. His daughter Marjorie Smith inherited the crystals, keeping a large one in a safety deposit vault in Bend. She allowed photographs for the 1971 *Gold Annual Magazine*.

Over the years, other seekers have tried and failed to find the cave opening. The cave could be a major tourist attraction, like the Oregon Caves National Monument, worth over $1 million after the installation of lights and pathways. But the main glory would be the fame and knowledge in rediscovering a geological treasure. Geologists knowledgeable of the region believe the calcite cave can exist near the contact zone of the high lava plains, along with an old marine formation where calcium formations and water exists. They believe this is definitely an area to search for the Lost Crystal Cave and that the cave is real because Marjorie Smith inherited the crystals.

HINTON CREEK CACHE

Just five miles east of Heppner, the county seat of Morrow County, is a scattered cache of $36,000 worth of gold coins along the banks of the North Fork of Hinton Creek, now called Kilkinney Creek. The site of the treasure is now on the Kilkinney Ranch, operated by Don Greenup in the 1950s.

Greenup constructed an earthen dam around 1950 for irrigation and livestock watering one mile above the ranch on the North Fork of Hinton Creek. The fill mainly came from the area where the old rancher's shop and cooler had stood for years. The pond behind the earthen dam was neither large nor deep. It was ideal to stock with fish and to use for swimming.

One angler from Heppner found a twenty-dollar gold piece in water about one foot deep, lying there within easy reach. There were rumors of other people finding double eagles. While swimming and digging sand along the water's edge, Greenup's sons found five five-dollar gold pieces.

The gold coins came to rest there as a result of the work of bulldozers. They moved the cache of coins where the old cooler house and shop once stood on the south bank of the creek. This explains how the coins ended up at the bottom of the pond, when the earth scrapers took off about two feet of dirt from the south bank. The lost coins may be in the fill of the dam, which is fifty yards long and twelve to fourteen feet deep at its highest point, or under the remainder at the old dugout site.

MITCHELL STAGE ROBBERY

Henry H. Wheeler, the owner of an Oregon stage line, carried gold from Baker City and Canyon City to The Dalles in 1864 when he was hired by Wells Fargo. Native Americans ambushed the stage in a narrow canyon near Mitchell, Oregon, on September 7, 1866. Wheeler was carrying $10,000 in greenbacks, $300 in coins, diamond rings and other valuables, according to H.S. Nedrey.

Wheeler was mistakenly shot in the mouth by Wells Fargo agents. One agent cut the two lead horses from the four-horse stage, and they rode west to near the Burnt Ranch, where Wheeler and the agent met men who quickly organized a posse to pursue the Native Americans. At the robbery site, the posse discovered that the Native Americans had taken all the gold but left the paper money. The Native American thieves did not realize the value of greenbacks and demolished the stagecoach.

Picture Gorge and US Highway 26, John Day River. *Author's photo.*

Eastern approach to Picture Gorge of the John Day River. *Author's photo.*

Wheeler and the agent were ambushed and rode north to The Dalles, where Wheeler received medical care. No one knows what happened to the loot. The posse arrived so quickly that the robbers could not have taken the bounty far, as the canyon walls are so narrow and steep. It could be somewhere in the steep canyon east of Mitchell, where today a monument two miles east of Mitchell in Wheeler County marks the spot. The Native Americans got away with the gold. I include this true story for those interested in Oregon history and treasure hunters.

Mitchell Monument

H.H. WHEELER
FOR WHICH WHEELER COUNTY WAS NAMED
FIRST PRESIDENT OF
EAST OREGON PIONEER ASSOCIATION.
ALSO MAIL CARRIER FROM
THE DALLES TO CANYON CITY
WAS ATTACKED NEAR THIS SPOT
BY INDIANS, WAS WOUNDED, MAIL
LOOTED AND COACH DESTROYED SEPT. 7, 1866.

6

SOUTHERN OREGON

SADDLE HORN GOLD

Victor Ingman met an ancient prospector in a Portland tavern in 1947. The old miner told a vivid story of a small valley of placer gold in Southern Oregon, and Ingman decided to head south immediately to the town of Rogue River. The old man was too frail to attempt the trip, but he gave Ingman specific directions and drew a map of the area that would lead to his valley of gold.

The old miner may have been a son or nephew of Charles L. Schieffelin, who lived in Washington County. In 1893, Schieffelin bought two mining claims: Delusion and Phantom Quartz. Both claims are located to the east of the left-hand fork of Foots Creek, one and a half miles above George Lance's cabin near the trail to the Middle Fork of Foots Creek. Charles sold the mining claims to his brother Ed, the discoverer of Tombstone, Arizona, and its mines, for $1,200 in 1895. Ed also bought two quartz prospects from family friends Alex and Jane Orme. Ed died while residing on Days Creek on May 12, 1897, and the claims passed to his brothers Eff, Jay and Charles and Ed's wife, Mary. The Schieffelin family wrote letters and maps on their mining activities and passed this information on to their sons and nephews.

A map showed a path up the Left Fork of Foots Creek, a ranger station and a lake with a saddleback mountain with a saddle horn formation protruding from one side of the peak. Once there, a searcher had to climb the mountain

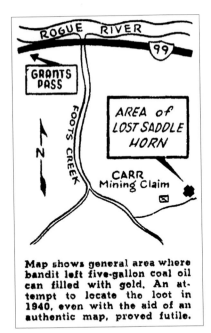

Map shows general area where bandit left five-gallon coal oil can filled with gold. An attempt to locate the loot in 1940, even with the aid of an authentic map, proved futile.

Lost Saddle Horn cache and mine. Oregonian *February 22, 1948, page 71.*

to the top and descend over the horn formation to the base of the mountain far below, where there was a little valley containing gold.

The sixty-year-old Ingman persuaded a companion to join his trek, and the pair headed south to the Rogue River. They went up the Left Fork of Foots Creek, past the Little Giant Mine by way of Horn Gulch, and had no problem finding the ranger station and lake. From the lake, they saw the saddleback mountain and its saddle horn formation.

Descending the mountainside from the horn proved to be sheer hell, and they barely survived their downward slide. The hillside was a rock slope, nearly vertical in places, with boulders as big as automobiles. The only way for them to descend was by sliding and grasping bushes and grass clumps to break their fall. At the bottom, they found a valley as indicated on the map. But instead of being a lush oasis, it contained boulders as big as houses. It was apparent to Ingman that a part of the mountain had slid down, covering the valley since the last time the old miner had been there. It was futile to dig or look for gold. The climb out of the valley proved much more difficult than the descent. Clawing their way up, Ingman and his partner jettisoned all their equipment, including blankets, shovels, picks, gold pans, extra clothes and, finally, their flashlights. They consumed all their remaining food so they would not have to carry it up, thus saving energy.

Ingman called it the worst ordeal of his life. "When we got back to where we had parked the car, I threw my arms around the automobile and kissed it," he said.

When Ingman returned to Portland, he told his story to Lloyd Frederickson and his sister-in-law, Katherine, of the Anglers Hotel in Nehalem, Oregon. Lloyd had almost gone with Ingman on his quest but was glad he did not. Later, Vic Ingram bragged how he managed to come out of the wilderness alive, comparing it to his time in the navy during World War II. Making his way back to Portland became his favorite story to tell until his death in 1951.

The Foots Creek drainage, named for prospector O.G. Foot, is a good place to look for gold. One of the first successful steam-powered dredges operated on Foots Creek in 1903. There are three mines located less than two miles to the northwest of the Left Fork of the creek: the Tinpan, Kubli and Ray. The Ray Mine, or Fair View Claim, at the three-thousand-foot elevation produced $9,000 from a pocket in 1934 and 1935. This could also be the claim that Inman heard about in 1947 from the old prospector, as its discovery date is not known.

While hiking on the Left Fork in 1947, Ingman met Ed Prefontaine and his family, who had lived on the Carr mining claim since the early 1930s. Prefontaine remembered a tall older man, Anton Baker, who came searching for gold in November 1931, driving up in a Model A Ford. Baker searched the area around a grove of madrona trees below the old mine shaft but gave up the search. It was not known what Baker was looking for, although it appeared that he was prospecting in a dry gulch behind the house, digging among the madrona trees.

A man and woman asked Mrs. Prefontaine in 1940 if she recalled Anton Baker's 1931 visit. Baker had died two months earlier in a Eugene hospital.

Rocker box gold-mining device. *Southern Oregon Historical Society No. 020763.*

The couple had worked as attendants in the hospital and helped with Baker's care. Before his death, Baker revealed that he had buried gold in a gulch under a madrona tree, which was marked with the carving of an old saddle horn where it first branched. Baker drew them a map.

The gold was from a stagecoach robbery near the town of Rogue River. Baker had hidden the gold in the 1880s after killing his two partners and burying their bodies in an old mine shaft, hoping to return after the law forgot about him. The return never happened, because Baker became an inmate in a California prison for killing a man in Sacramento. He was unable to return to recover the gold until he was extremely old.

Prefontaine became excited, because he remembered seeing an old, rusty saddle horn perched in the first branches of a madrona tree among a grove of the trees below the old mine shaft in a nearby gulch. He believed the real Saddle Horn Gold was not a mine but a cache. Together, the threesome located the mineshaft, which had partly caved in, thus hiding the two bodies. Below the mineshaft, they searched for days among a forest of madrona trees but failed to find the one marked with a saddle horn as remembered by Prefontaine. Prefontaine concluded that the saddle horn had simply rusted away.

In 1934, Ed Prefontaine found a piece of quartz on Foots Creek. It contained 13.63 ounces of gold. Ed tried to uncover the valley of gold, and he also continued to search over the years for the Saddle Horn cache.

In the early 1950s, he bought a metal detector, hoping this would aid his search for additional gold nuggets as well as help him to find Baker's cache. Returning to the hillside, he found that a fire had ravaged the madrona grove, destroying all the trees. In addition, the fire and ensuing rain caused erosion from the hillside, covering the former grove with dirt and stream gravel so deep that his metal detector proved useless. Prefontaine never received a positive signal of metal in the hidden valley, nor did Vic Ingman. The tons of soil and rock on the valley floor hinder the range of metal detectors.

GALL CREEK CACHE

Gall Creek flows north to the Rogue River in Jackson County, across from the old town of Rock Point. This is gold-mining country, and gold claims exist along its banks. The gulch and cabin sites have grown up in brush in the ensuing years.

ROGUE RIVER AND UMPQUA VALLEYS.

Umpqua and Rogue River valleys. History of Oregon, *Volume 2 by Hubert Bancroft, 1888, page 380, author's copy.*

In the late 1870s, a young boy named Jake witnessed a fight between two brothers. These brothers traded their gold at Rock Point, where Ben Haymond ran a general store. He exchanged their gold for twenty-dollar gold pieces and supplies. They bought little besides coffee, flour and salt, because they ate deer meat and avoided the saloons and barbershop.

One of the mines is the Bill Nye claim, or Bee-Hive Mine, found around 1900. It had a northeast-striking vertical quartz vein two feet wide and a larger, northwest-striking vein of impure quartzite. Two shipments of ore from 1907 to 1909 totaled $12,000 in gold, which was extracted by a five-

Brown's mining cabin. *Southern Oregon Historical Society No. 13772.*

stamp mill. This formation is the source of placer mines along Gall Creek, with the Blockert Mine the most productive placer claim.

One of the brothers decided to build a new privy. He chose the location and began swinging his pick into the rocky ground. After four swings, his brother rushed toward him, trying to stop the excavation, because his buried gold was at the excavation site. The pick-swinging brother tried to stop him. The other brother ducked the weapon, drew his gun and fired, killing him.

It was a case of murder or self-defense; no one would know for sure. The survivor of the fight left his brother on the ground and returned to his cabin. Sometime after midnight, the survivor, feeling remorse and fearing a murder charge, committed suicide with his revolver.

A nearby prospector who heard the shots came by in the morning to investigate. He found the two dead brothers. He dug a shallow grave and laid the brothers side by side before contacting the sheriff. The only witness to the brothers' feud was young Jacob, who searched for the buried can of gold for years without success.

The Spencer Creek Cache

Granville Keene and partner J.Q. Faber ran a crooked card game in Yreka, California, in 1855. The pair tricked players and parted miners from their gold dust. Finally, ill feelings against them ran so high that the two gamblers decided in August 1855 to leave Yreka to prevent discovery of the bunco operation.

They traveled northeast with their ill-gotten winnings to Oregon. During this time, the only travelers were pioneers heading west on the Applegate Trail, the main migrant route into Southern Oregon. Rogue River Indians on Bear Creek wounded Faber and killed Keene near Keene Creek, which was later named for him.

The wounded J.Q. Faber fled east up the Klamath River to Spencer Creek, a stream that flows south to the Klamath River. The first settlers on Spencer Creek were the Grubb family. The Grubbs remained in the area, ending with family burials in a private graveyard near the original homestead overlooking the Klamath River one half mile south of the mouth of Spenser Creek, where a Grubb daughter married a member of the Spenser clan.

A female medium residing on upper Spencer Creek convinced neighbor E.W. Barham, a trapper living on Buck Lake, of the location of $30,000 in lost gold. According to the seer, the cache was less than four miles east of Keno near a culvert on Highway 66.

Barham believed the woman, but by 1934, at age sixty-four, he was too infirm to search by himself. Hal H. Ogle rescued Barham in January 1923, when he nearly died of starvation and gangrene. Ogle transported Barham to a Klamath Falls hospital, where doctors amputated both of his feet. Barham returned home to his wife and three children at Medford.

Later, Ogle visited Barham in Medford to see how he was recovering and met the spiritualist from Spenser Creek. She proclaimed Ogle "a guardian angel." Barham later moved to California, and Ogle did not see him again until 1934.

The old trapper reappeared at the Pelican Hotel in Klamath Falls. Barham asked Ogle to go on a treasure hunt, paying Ogle $29,000. Barham would keep $1,000. Ogle refused to help in the dubious search. Meanwhile, the medium convinced others that there was gold buried in the Grubb family plot.

Through the years, rumors persisted that the Yreka gamblers buried their gold under one of the Grubb family tombstones, because the graveyard was on a prominent hill. The Grubb family members witnessed nighttime digging occurring under tombstones and found fresh holes in their graveyard, even though the gamblers' flight happened years before the first burial. It is important to emphasize that gold buried along the banks of the Klamath River or the eleven-mile length of Spencer Creek is not in local graveyards or family burial plots.

UPPER ROGUE RIVER CACHES

In the 1860s, six gold slugs worth $300 were lost in the waters of the Rogue River, about five miles upstream from Grants Pass at Hunters Ferry, where the old migrant road crosses the river. An unidentified man leaned over the rail of the Hunters Ferry. His purse, which he carried in the breast pocket of his woolen shirt, fell into the Rogue River. Searches were conducted in the deep water, but all efforts to recover just one gold slug failed. The six gold slugs, weighing two and a half ounces each, lay at the bottom of the Rogue River. They are worth almost $4,000 each at current gold prices.

JOEL PERKINS

Joel Perkins, the founder of Lafayette, Oregon, in 1842 buried a cache of gold dust on his property. He was a miner and prospector going to the California gold fields in 1848. He later lived on the Rogue River, where he operated a ferry above White Rocks, now a short distance east, where the municipal railroad bridge is today, just beyond the eastern city limits of Grants Pass.

Perkins was murdered at the age of twenty-six by Jonathan Malone while returning from California on the south slope of the Siskiyou Mountains on July 24, 1856. The murder was over a dispute over Perkins's wife, Laura.

No one saw the gold dust Perkins earned as a ferryboat operator, because he never used a bank, unlike pioneers of the era. Early settlers usually buried their money. Perkins's buried gold should be near the former ferry landing slip at White Rocks.

LOST SACKS OF GOLD NUGGETS

The gold discovery on the small north-flowing Homestead Creek, which flows into Williams Creek near the community of Williams, started a local rush in Josephine County. The Harrison and Jones brothers, with the help of a Native American called "Lum the Monument Maker," took out $2,000 a day in almost pure gold, as reported in the *Rogue River Courier* on May 22, 1908.

"The first panful we took out of that pocket ran $700," said Ben Harrison, one of the discoverers of the gold pocket. "That's a lot of gold, and as we swung our picks into the steep hillside, the gold nuggets would rattle down the bank to our feet,"

The older brother, Robert, later gathered $800 in gold in one pan of dirt. Residents decided after reading the newspaper accounts and seeing the trips the pair made to the bank to help themselves to the brothers' gold. Dozens of patrons of the William saloon, fired up by liquor, marched one June night in 1908 with their lanterns, picks, shovels and canvas sacks. They walked three miles uphill northeast toward the rich pocket.

Ben Harrison; Lum, an elderly Native American; and one of the Jones brothers panicked when they saw the parade of people waving lanterns, candles and torches coming toward them in the middle of the night. The approaching line looked like a two-hundred-foot-long luminous snake crashing through the brush, interspaced with yelling, singing and laughing. Harrison, Lum and the brothers debated whether to stop and bury all the gold already uncovered or just scoop it all up.

It did not matter, because five minutes later, the drunken mob had surrounded them on the slope, upslope and downhill. Empty whiskey bottles containing nuggets rolled down the slopes. Everyone was finding gold and putting it into sacks. Men were carrying the sacks over their shoulders back to Williams.

Then one of the half dozen and sober residents yelled, "What should we do with it?"

"Bury the sacks downhill, away thereby the bush pile," answered Harrison.

Jones appointed Lum to oversee the operation by handing out eleven sacks to Lum. Lum was too old and overwhelmed trying to know where the sacks were. When dawn's early light broke, there was a barren hillside with no one in sight except Jones, Lum and Harrison. There was lots of gold lying around.

"Oh, well," said Harrison. "What do we care if those fellows did get away with lot of gold last night? There is still much gold left."

The threesome gathered up over $16,000 in gold. How much the townspeople carried off could not be determined. Their attention then turned to the eleven seamless sacks that had been handed out by Lum for burial. Harrison found five sacks buried near the downhill row of bushes

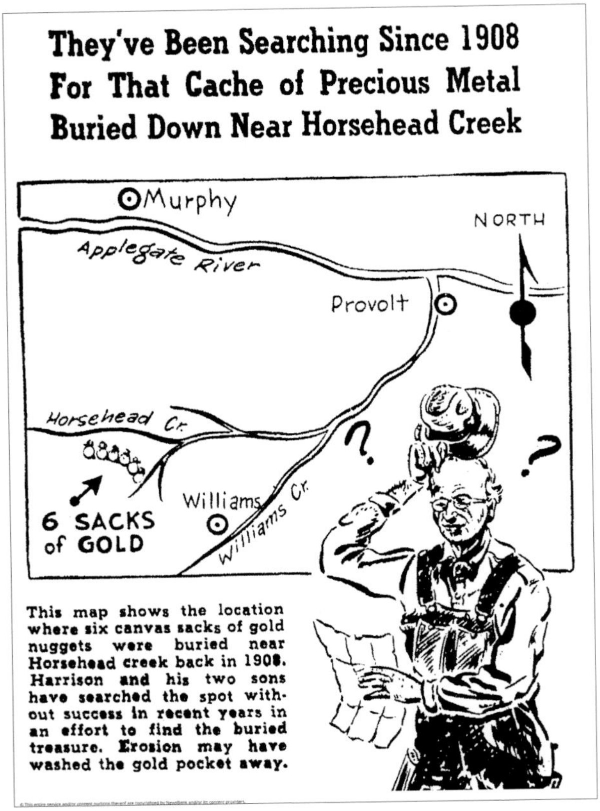

They've Been Searching Since 1908
For That Cache of Precious Metal
Buried Down Near Horsehead Creek

⊙Murphy

NORTH

Applegate River

Provolt ⊙

Horsehead Cr.

6 SACKS
of GOLD

Williams Cr.

Williams ⊙

This map shows the location where six canvas sacks of gold nuggets were buried near Horsehead creek back in 1908. Harrison and his two sons have searched the spot without success in recent years in an effort to find the buried treasure. Erosion may have washed the gold pocket away.

Sketch of Benjamin
Harrison and map of bags
of gold nuggets. Oregonian,
October 12, 1947, page 67.

seventy feet uphill from a small stream that is a tributary of Horsehead Creek. Further searching to uncover the six remaining sacks failed.

Forty years later, in 1947, Ben Harrison returned with his two grown sons to look for the gold at the site of the old pocket. They were hoping to find the pocket by panning for gold and to uncover the six sacks of misplaced nuggets. The gold deposit could not be located, even after a week of intensive searching.

The ground had eroded and logging taken place. New roads and fences further confused Harrison as to where the exact spot was. Ben Harrison gave up the search and retired from mining to live in a small cabin on Foots Creek in Jackson County, Oregon, where Dale Vincent from the *Oregonian* interviewed him in October 1947. Where a row of bushes once grew there now exist six small caches of gold nuggets spread out in the ground. They await recovery with the aid of a modern metal detector.

SWAN LAKE CACHE

S.K. Ogle of Klamath Falls, Oregon, heard about an old tale of treasure. He decided to enlist the help of his twenty-year-old son, Hal, who owned a motorcycle. Together, they rode out to Swan Lake, with the older Ogle hanging on to his son on the back of the motorcycle. In the dry fields, they located the decaying log foundations of a former post office. The twosome followed the rumored directions: ninety paces forward and then nine paces back, then three paces north. There, S.K. almost fell into a gaping hole.

"Damn, somebody's beat us to it," said S.K. Ogle. "We might as well go home."

Years later, the middle-aged Hal H. Ogle was talking to Lloyd Lowe, a former sheriff, about his unsuccessful treasure hunt at Swan Lake and the big hole he had found with his father.

"Hey, I was the one who dug that big hole out there," said Low. "I heard the story and thought I would try it. But I did not find a thing; I can swear to that. If the gold was there, it would still be there for all of me."

Sheriff Lowe and the Ogle team were both searching in the wrong place, because there has never been a post office or stagecoach stop at Swan Lake Valley east of Klamath Falls. A farmer from California arrived in Klamath Falls around 1900 seeking information. He hired a ranch hand years before who became ill. The ranch hand confessed on his deathbed to his boss that he helped rob a stagecoach.

The old ranch hand narrated how he and his partner had successfully robbed the stage, which ran between Jacksonville, Oregon, and Yreka, California, of $12,000 in 1872. After the robbery, the two decided to separate, and the ranch hand took the gold with him. He promised he would meet his partner in California after the excitement died down.

In the hopes of throwing off any pursuers, the highwayman stopped at a cabin near a spring in the woods somewhere in the Swan Lake Valley to spend the night. At this location, the owner often took in lodgers and delivered mail for hire by horseback from Klamath Falls to Sprague River. A nearby spring provided water for the cabin owner to grow hay for his ponies and potatoes. He lived there with his son and a hired hand, who took care of the ponies in an adjoining shelter. This mail delivery system ended when a murder took place in a Klamath Falls saloon. The mail carrier disappeared with his son and the hired hand to the east.

The stagecoach bandit grew restless and paranoid, fearing a posse was about to swoop down from the hills and catch him and all the gold. The

Miners at Sterling Mine. *Southern Oregon Historical Society #00309.*

solution was to rid himself of the stolen gold. Then he would be safe enough and could later come back for it.

In the middle of the night, he woke. He exited the cabin through the back door and paced 190 steps east, where he started to bury the gold. He hit a rock. He realized that he was in a potato patch. He walked 9 steps back, then 3 steps north, where he found a soft spot and buried the loot.

The next day, he left for California. He decided not to meet his partner and never returned to Oregon for the gold. He worked as a miner, turned respectable and later worked as a full-time ranch hand, forgetting the gold he had left behind in the potato patch.

Treasure seekers have sought the gold around abandoned cabins in the vicinity of Swan Lake. One old cabin had a rock fireplace. In the flue of the chimney, a previous party of searchers uncovered old augers.

Captain O.C. Applegate searched for the buried treasure in 1908. He knew the location of the original cabin, which had burned down on the road to Swan Lake. From the depression marking the site of the old cabin, he went west, to the place where a fence once stood delineating the potato patch. Then he stepped 220 paces into the woods and up a hill, where there were four trees, as mentioned in the written description.

Turning around to these four trees to face the old cabin site, O.C. Applegate paced nine steps, then stepped abruptly to the right and dug two feet into one of the hardest beds of natural hardpan ever encountered. He found nothing. Applegate said in summary, "That splendid collection of double eagles remains somewhere in the bosom of Klamath County, doing nobody any good."

NORTHEASTERN OREGON

BEAR CREEK MINE

In 1882, a railroad tie cutting crew was camping near the homestead of William H. Jarboe fifteen miles north of Elgin in the extreme northern part of Union County. The five laborers from just across the Oregon-Washington boundary were on their way to work for the Great Northern Railroad. While they were traversing an old Native American trail along McIntyre Ridge, dusk was approaching. The fivesome turned off the trail and went into a canyon to camp for the night.

At dawn, they decided to take a shorter path to the railroad tie camp by trekking up the canyon, crossing the mountain ridge or divide from Bear Creek and then going down to Jarboe Meadow at 4,068 feet. One of the men noticed a colored ledge in the canyon wall. He, along with companions who were knowledgeable about mining, chipped samples of the colored rock to take with them when they returned home to Walla Walla. After spending the summer at the railroad work camp, they sought the advice of an assayer. The men read the report in a state of near shock.

The assay report showed an incredible content of 26 percent copper, 18 percent silver and 37 percent gold, making the find worth $90,000 a ton. The men had to wait until spring to journey out of town to find the canyon containing metal ore, because the ledge was located just below the five-thousand-foot elevation level. The five men and their partners searched for years but were never able to relocate the rich outcropping.

In the fall of 1884, a band of Indians rode into Joseph, carrying a comrade mauled by a bear in the mountains. John Henry Williams believed the Natives had found gold and decided to find it by backtracking the Indians' trail. High in the Wallowa Mountains, Williams and the other searchers found their campsite alongside a lake, but there the trail vanished.

A sheepherder who had no interest in mining may have found the same mineral outcropping again in 1900. He had picked up rocks to ward off bears. Other sheepherders had flocks in the area, and the camp cook brought food and supplies to all of them.

The shepherd, employed by Judge Chester F. Miller of Dayton, Washington, took the rocks from his pockets and tossed them near the campfire one evening while all of the sheepherders were gathering around their tents. The camp cook, who was interested in prospecting, picked up the rocks to examine them.

When asked by the cook where he found the bright stones, the herder said he had immediately noticed the rocks containing gold while picking up and pocketing the stones out of a creek; he heard a noise and glanced up, utterly terrified seeing nine bears above the creek banks. He used the larger rocks to get away by throwing them into the bushes to distract the hungry animals. After more questioning, the herder promised to show the cook the location. But it was late fall, and by the next morning, a snowstorm had occurred. The herders were forced to take the sheep to another meadow at a lower elevation. The cook and herder never had time to trek back to the ledge.

After arriving at home, the cook took the specimens to Judge Miler, who received the same rich report the railroad workers had received in Walla Walla eighteen years before. The sheepherder died before springtime, and the cook was never able to find the rich ledge. The creek where the sheepherder viewed a record nine bears at one time became known as Bear Creek.

No rich gold ore exists north of Jarboe Creek near Bear Creek, which flows into the Grande Ronde River. A knowledgeable prospector or lucky bear hunter in either Union or Wallowa County may locate the ledge, now known as the Lost Bear Creek Mine.

Wallowa Gold

Henri Sebastian, eighty-one, trekked up the Lostine River into the Wallowa Mountains in search of Native American gold. He carried a map and written notes, which he often consulted. The map directions were as follows:

NEZ PERCÉS CAMP OF CHIEF JOSEPH AT NESPELEM, WASHINGTON, WHERE HE DIED IN 1904

"Nez Perce Camp," 1904, at Nespelem, Washington. History of the Oregon Country *by Harvey Scott, 1924, page 211, author's copy.*

south alongside the Lostine River to the East Lostine River, then east across Hurricane Divide and up again to the lowest point between Sacajawea Peak and the Matterhorn. It is not known if Sebastian was seeking a Nez Perce cache or a gold mine.

His good friend, John Cash-Cash, a Nez Perce tribe member and local rancher, had purchased all his tracts of ranch land with gold and then disappeared into the Wallowa Mountains. He recounted the oral accounts of Native American gold to Sebastian. Cash died only a week earlier, passing the secret of the gold to Sebastian, who had pledged not to seek the gold as long as Cash lived. Three weeks after Cash died, Sebastian returned to the town of Joseph and bought mining tools, food and all the cigars and costly European wines the store had in stock. The Frenchman paid for these items by drawing out nuggets containing gold from his leather poke.

When the clerk measured out the gold on a scale, ranchers and Native Americans looked on with awe. Sebastian had found either a rich gold mine or the cache of the Nez Perce gold rumored to be somewhere in the Wallowa Mountains. Sebastian found the lost Bear Creek Mine, rumored to be on the stream just west of the Lostine River drainage instead of near the other Bear Creek, located more than twenty miles to the north, flowing into the Grande Ronde River.

Henri Sebastian trekked up the Lostine River two days later, telling locals he would be back in a month. Weeks later, a Nez Perce member was in possession of Sebastian's horse and saddle. The Native American disappeared and was never questioned about how he obtained Sebastian's horse, if he knew anything about the eighty-year-old miner's disappearance and if he knew whether Sebastian had died of natural causes or was murdered.

There was a reported landslide in the Lostine Canyon, sixteen miles south of the town of Lostine, which may have buried Sebastian and the native gold mine. The sole survivor of the slide was Sebastian's horse, which somehow escaped the rock and mud of the landslide. Other local Native Americans were no help in illuminating Sebastian's fate. They only said that spirits watch over the gold. A Nez Perce medicine man put a curse on the gold, which became off-limits to all tribal members. Within a year, Nez Perce members no longer traded gold at local stores. One quarter mile north of the U.S. Forest Service Shady Camp campground, the remnants of the slide are still evident across the Lostine River.

F.B. Earley, along with the nephew of Chief Joseph, Red Thunder, attempted to find the source of the Nez Perce gold. They left the town of Lostine in the spring of 1908. The high snows of the Wallowa Mountains stopped their first attempt. In the fall, they tried again. This search ended when Red Thunder fell off his horse and suffered a severe injury, preventing any further searching that year. Natives stated that the injury was a result of Chief Joseph's curse, which guarded the gold and prevented discovery by anyone outside of the tribe.

The legend of the Lost Bear Mine started in 1884, when a small band of Nez Perce members rode into the town of Joseph carrying an injured tribal member mauled by a bear. Hearing the talk surrounding this bear attack, John Henry Wilson determined that the Indigenous hunters had been at their gold mine and left Joseph to find it. He and locals followed the Native American trail to a lake where the Natives had camped but lost the trail. Wilson searched for years but never discovered anything of value.

Sebastian may have discovered the lost mine rumored to exist on 9,839-foot Sacajawea Peak or the cave of stored Nez Perce gold located fifty yards north of the lowest point of the one-and-a-half-mile saddle between the 10,004-foot Matterhorn and Sacajawea Peak. Nez Perce members traveled past Chief Joseph Mountain to the high lakes, where they hunted and gathered berries before returning to the Wallowa Valley with gold nuggets to trade.

Mountain climbers found the vertical entrance of a thirty-foot cave but no gold. Sebastian must have removed all the stashed gold from the cave and hidden it elsewhere. Additionally, two separate parties of gold prospectors, a four-man party from California and another from the Pacific Northwest, combed the Wallowa Mountains in the 1970s but found no gold. A lost gold mine, if it does exist, would lie below seven thousand feet, like the Cornucopia Mines and the Eagle Creek Mining District fifteen miles to the south, which may be the true source of the Nez Perce gold, not on the higher slopes of Matterhorn or Sacajawea Peak.

LOST GOLD OF BIG SINK

The Big Sink is located approximately two miles southeast of Jubilee Lake in Union County. Both Sinks—Little and Big—were known unofficially by local settlers as the Devils Sinks. Ironically, Little Sink is the larger of the two and is located just to the northeast of the misnamed Big Sink. Both Sinks are accessible by hiking from Forest Road 63 on Sinks Trail No. 3233. From above, the area appears as though a three-mile horseshoe-shaped piece of ground had sunk into the earth.

Enhancing the mystery is that compass readings do not always point to magnetic north, causing early explorers to become lost and frightened, thus the nickname "Devil Sinks." The eastern side of The Sinks is at 4,165 feet and is rimmed with large ponderosa pines. Looking west, the ground drops 100 feet to a 300-foot cliff with a field of twenty-ton boulders at its base lying on a thin layer of lava.

In 1908, an elderly Nez Perce member known as Garguash arrived at an Elgin mercantile to buy food. When the storekeeper inquired where he found his gold, Garguash said he had dug it from a shallow depression in The Sinks. He was nonchalant in relating the source of his gold, because he knew no white man could find it in The Sinks area, located eighteen miles north of Elgin.

Garguash paid his entire bill with gold nuggets and left the store, heading back to camp. His tribe always set up their camp near the slopes of a natural dam situated at the lower end of the Little Sink. As Garguash walked along the path home, the earthen dam suddenly burst, unleashing a torrent of water and killing the residents of Garguash's village. From then on, all of the survivors except Garguash avoided the entire area of The Sinks. Local prospectors, after hearing the tale, tried to track the wily old man. Garguash always eluded them.

But ten years before, a sawmill operator had found the gold. He worked at a mill located at the confluence of Motet Creek and Little Looking Glass Creek. The worker was heading home for a visit, entering the area of The Sinks, and became lost. Darkness approached, forcing the mill hand to spend the night. He found a protected spot next to a small ledge.

At dawn, he noticed that someone had been digging in the ledge, which contained quartz and gold. He took a large sample after camouflaging the ledge and then headed west to his family home in Weston, fifteen miles away in Umatilla County. His family was overjoyed, because the hardworking mill hand had finally had good fortune, finding a gold mine and the source of the legendary Nez Perce gold.

Their joy did not last. While walking around the farm, the mill hand fell and broke his hip and was unable to trek back to The Sinks. The hip injury left him disabled, and he had to rely on his son to uncover the quartz ledge, giving detailed instructions to the son on how to recognize and uncover it.

The son returned to The Sinks. He never found gold or even quartz in the area despite searching for years. He eventually grew too old to search. The golden ledge that the worker's son failed to find and that Garguash left behind remains to this day somewhere in the jumbled terrain of The Sinks.

SHEEPHERDER'S LOST GOLD MINE

In 1918, a sheepherder claimed to have discovered a gold-studded ledge in Union County. All of the previously discovered mines are located to the south in Baker County, outside the Eagle Cap Wilderness Area. The sheepherder did not know until months had passed what he had discovered on that little knoll overlooking a small meadow on Eagle Creek.

The Eagle Creek Mining District is home to over ten gold mines, where quartz veins in shale and mudstones occur in the Upper Triassic Hurwal Formation, in a sequence of argillite laminated siltstone, sandstone and shale with minor limestone, chert and conglomerate. The most profitable mine was the Sanger Mine, or Summit Lode, where production occurred from 1870 to 1897. The Sanger Mine is located on a branch of Goose Creek, near the summit of the Powder River-Eagle Creek Divide two and a half miles west of Eagle Creek.

The Mother Lode Mine on Balm Creek produced a much smaller amount of gold in three years beginning in 1935. Production from five other lode deposits was even smaller. They are the Basin, East Eagle, Amalgamated,

Lilly White and Dolly Varden deposits. The Basin Mine is located two miles west of West Eagle Creek and is the northernmost of the known lode discoveries. Placer deposits along Eagle Creek occur in the heavy gravels one hundred feet above current stream level from just below the mouth of Paddy Creek three or more miles and upstream above the mouth of East Eagle Creek. The Shanghai and Town Gulches drain northeast into Eagle Creek. In addition, sections of both Paddy and East Eagle Creeks have placer gold.

The Big Vein at the head of Fir Gulch may have been source of the rich placers on Fir Gulch. The Eagle Creek placer and lode mining occurred before the twenty-two-mile ditch was completed from West Eagle Creek to Sparta in 1873.

The alleged sheepherder discovery is north of these major areas of mining and lies in the upper drainage of Eagle Creek in the Wallowa batholith of the late Jurassic to Early Cretaceous ages. The discovery was to the north of all reported mining of both lode and placer claims. Access by motor and use of mechanized equipment is prohibited in all wilderness areas.

Mineral deposits in the wilderness area occur in zones of thermal alteration or metamorphic deposits lying between granite and calcareous sediments,

Wallowa gold miners. *Oregon Historical Society No. 38194.*

where granitic rocks intruded. Gold and silver deposits are present in little more than trace amounts, according to the Oregon Department of Geology and Mineral Industries. For this reason alone, I believe the location of a rich gold discovery by a sheepherder in 1918 on upper Eagle Creek is a myth. The discovery, if true, was a low-level prospect located outside of the Eagle Creek Wilderness Area.

WILLOW SPRINGS CACHE

In the 1890s, a longtime resident of Willow Springs, ten miles south of Pilot Rock, invited travelers by horseback and wagon to eat and spend the night. Willow Springs was just off the stage route and was not a regular stop or watering hole. It lay in a deep pocket just yards off the trail. The odd thing about this man was that he told guests he had hidden money. He would then go outside, be gone for three minutes and return with his leather bag filled with $4,000 in gold coins.

His friends tried to talk him out of showing the money to just anybody who stopped by. He responded that nobody would ever find his gold and that he would rather die than give up his treasure. Then, a fire occurred on his property. His body was found in the ashes of his wood shack. It was never determined if he died from the smoke and heat of the fire, nor was it determined if someone committed arson to hide a hideous crime.

The money went missing. The bounty must still be under a rock or other landmark only a short distance from the site of the old cabin. People have searched the homestead, including writer Paul Atkinson, and there is no public record of its discovery.

The Willow Springs Canyon is located on Bear Creek on the northern slopes of Battle Mountain State Park in Umatilla County. It was a common watering hole for travelers using the Pendleton–John Day Trail and the site of an Indigenous skirmish during the Bannock Indian War on July 8, 1878.

W.J. BENNETT CACHE

William J. Bennett, Union County resident and ex-convict, rebuilt his life after a receiving a pardon by the Oregon governor from a life sentence for killing a neighbor. He lived alone in a small house on the southeastern slope of Mount Sinai, where he grew crops and raised horses. The horse-raising made Bennett so rich that he accumulated $20,000 in $20 gold coins, or double eagles.

During his senior years, he befriended the young son of a neighbor, Lynn Hill, drafted in 1918 by the U.S. Army. In 1902, Bennett told the young Hill that he buried all his gold coins on his land near his home. He asked Lynn if he would like to see the $10,000 in gold he just received from the sale of horses. When Lynn said he would, Bennett took four canvas sacks from the saddle roll and poured their contents onto a saddle blanket on the ground. Each bag held 125 gold pieces.

The elderly Bennett wanted Hill to recover the money so that if he was dead, the young soldier could give the majority portion of his estate to his deaf daughter, Belle. He gave Hill directions to his cache and urged Hill to keep a portion for himself. Lynn Hill was to go to the north window of the Bennett house and look directly at a small hill known locally as Mount Sinai. He was then to walk two hundred yards directly toward the hill and turn right, then walk to a flat rock beside a bush, where groundhogs had dug. In a crevice of the flat rock was wedged an iron ring of a wagon axle shaft or bolen thirty to forty feet away and to the northeast of this rock marker, $20,000 in gold coins was buried under a big rock in a binder-twin box and a crock jar.

Lynn Hall returned from the Great War and found out that Bennett had died. Hall searched the south side of the hill, failing to find even the flat rock containing the wagon axle ring. Other searchers heard of the treasure. They tore down the Bennett house and dug holes around it. Only about $1,100 in small gold and silver coins were recovered.

There is no record of the uncovering of the remainder of Bennett's buried gold among the two poplar trees, apple trees, scattered rocks of the house foundation, barn and old well of the homestead. Treasure searcher and writer Randy Simmons in 1975 found square nails, horseshoes, a knife and spoon, a chain, parts of an old frying pan and lids from old baking soda tins. But zero gold coins.

The problem of locating the Bennett homestead is that Mount Sinai is not on current maps. It is a hill known locally, somewhere at the northern end of the Grande Rhonde Valley, where the Grande Rhonde River flows through a rocky gorge. Bennett constructed a large barn in 1872, and it was reported still standing in 1978. It is a key in locating the Bennett homestead.

Stage Gulch Road

Stage Gulch Road runs twenty miles west from Pendleton Airport to the eastern boundary of the town of Stanfield. In the early 1900s, a stagecoach robbery occurred halfway between the towns. The loot was about $1,200 in gold. The next day in Sanford, the highwaymen confessed and were later hanged for theft.

One of the bandits, trying to bargain, yelled that the gold was in Stage Gulch, buried near the location of the holdup. It may still be there, at Umatilla Meadows, approximately ten miles between both towns along Stage Gulch Road.

There has been gold discovered along Stage Gulch Road at the Branstitter Ranch. The chickens at the ranch had at one time gold in their craws. Also, there were rumors of quail and pheasants found with flakes of gold in their claws.

Brian Branstitter told writer Paul Atkinson in 1963 that when word first leaked about the gold in the chickens' craws, his family was besieged by people wanting information about the source of the gold supply and whether it was natural or from the torn sacks buried by stagecoach robbers. Nobody found much, and the gold fever died down. Since the gold appears not to be from a placer deposit, it is part of the stolen stagecoach money buried in a shallow hole and scattered by the winds and rains when the canvas bags rotted away.

There is another story associated with Stage Gulch Road, dating from 1880. A Wells Fargo employee, who received $500 a month in salary, was arrested for robbery. On the day of the robbery, Page, an inspector posing as a passenger, rode the stage to Sanford and beyond to Umatilla Landing and eventually to Portland. He started the trip sitting beside the driver. In his inspection tours of the Utah, Idaho and Oregon Stage Company, he often drank heavily and went on drunken sprees. He became drowsy and went to nap in the stagecoach boot, which is a cozy, quiet place. The mail bags made a comfortable bed among the strongboxes for a tired traveler on the Concord coach. Price, as an inspector, always had the keys.

When the stagecoach reached its destination, the strongbox and its contents were missing. Wells Fargo agents backtracked along the route, searching for evidence of the robbery. In a shed near the Prospect Farm stage station across from Stage Gulch, they found where the division of the loot took place. The agents found papers thrown across the shed, piles of burnt matches and ripped waybills.

Page was in Portland, and he returned Pendleton to stand trial. He had extracted a $150 gold watch and other valuable articles, which he sold to a Portland pawn shop. He had a beautiful young wife, an infant son and friends and stood high in business and fraternal circles. The evidence was mostly circumstantial, leading to his acquittal, allowing him to leave Oregon.

The people of Umatilla County believed that Page threw the strongbox contents to his confederates on Stage Gulch Road or at a designated location, where he hoped to return and recover the bounty. Page had the opportunity to recover the loot. After his arrest, he left his family to become a prospector in the Seven Devils Mountains of Idaho. One of his female friends remarked, "If he is a roaming in the Seven Devils Mountains that make eight devils there now."

He moved to Ellensburg, Washington, and later made a trip to Portland in 1889, staying at the International Hotel. That was the last of Page in the public press.

Baker Ranch Cache

Baker Ranch is located four miles south of the town of Pilot Rock, along the East Birch Creek Road on the left. Somewhere in the old cattle feed lies a can containing $1,000 in gold coins. Around 1900, William Baker decided the ground was the safest place for his savings. Like most people of his era, he did not trust the banks.

Baker placed the money in a can, then walked four yards from the house. There was a large tree on the east bank and a large rock on the west bank of East Birch Creek as markers. He buried his coins on the west side of the creek in a can of gold between the two landmarks, only five feet from the creek.

Later, East Birch Creek flooded, destroying everything in its path. The rock marker Baker discovered after the flood subsided is on the west bank of East Birch Creek. The marker had either been washed away or covered in mud. The can was lost in the raging torrent.

Baker Sr.'s son Bill, who lived at the same ranch, remembered the tree marker on the east bank. The tree was cut down in 1965. He pointed out the location to treasure seekers, including Paul Atkinson of *True West* magazine. The can and gold coins have all scattered and remain lost.

RESERVATION RANCH CACHE

Kokoyealash, an elderly Native American woman, brought farming operations to a halt on the Umatilla Reservation in early March 1915. The proprietor, R.F. Kirkpatrick, who heard her treasure tale, had every hired hand on the ranch hunting for a buried can of gold.

In 1896, the middle-aged Native American woman cached a can of gold near her old tepee. She was too sick to be able to pinpoint the exact spot, giving up all hope of uncovering the buried can after a diligent search. She was driven by automobile back to her former homesite.

HELLS CANYON LOOT

A robbery of First National Bank of Joseph occurred on October 1, 1896. David Green Tucker had a finger shot off, one robber was killed and Si Fitzhugh escaped, riding eastward with $2,000. Homer Hayes, age nine at the time, related:

We were at school recess when these three guys came up. We thought they were Negroes because they had blackened up. But we never seen a Negro, so we didn't know. The school was just across the street from the bank. Next thing you know, we heard shots. You see, it was dividend day, and a lot of folks came to the bank to collect their money. The word went out

Beginning of the mighty Snake River Canyon, likened by one man who had viewed it to "Dante's Inferno." Beginning at a point about sixty miles south of Lewiston, and continuing well into southern Idaho, the Snake River has cut its way through the basaltic rock. This is the deepest river trench in America. In one place the floor of the river is 7,000 feet below the tips of the surrounding hills. In many places the walls of the canyon rear themselves perpendicularly above the water, forming what is known as "box" canyons. Powerful gasoline boats navigate this canyon, and it is a trip one never forgets. There are but two men, both residents of Lewiston, capable of piloting boats through this canyon.

Snake River Canyon. *From* River of No Return, *1947, by Robert G. Bailey, author's copy.*

Aerial view of Imnaha River Valley, the escape route of bank robber Si Fitzhugh to Snake River and into Idaho during 1896. *Author's photo, 1978.*

that the bank was being robbed and all the businessmen grabbed their guns and rushed out.

Well, these three guys ran from the bank to visit their horses. They vaulted to the saddle, but the guy with the money got shot off his horse and killed. His name was Brown. Another robber, Fitzhugh, jumped down and got the money sack and rode off.

David Tucker, sixteen, had his right index finger shot off when he held his hands up to surrender. An angry bank patron shot the gun trying to protect his life savings. It is not known why the posse failed to follow Si Fitzhugh

Hells Canyon, 1947. River of No Return, *1947, by Robert G. Bailey, page 664, author's copy.*

northeast out of Joseph to Little Sheep Creek upstream to a prairie where a fresh horse was available.

Later, Fitzhugh's trail led to the East Fork of Cow Creek, near Summit Ridge above Hells Canyon. Then he headed south, descending to the Imnaha River. Heading eastward, he crossed the Snake River into Idaho at Ballard's Landing. Most informed searchers believed Fitzhugh buried the $2,000 on the East Fork of Cow Creek and was killed before he could return to recover his cache above Hells Canyon.

EPILOGUE

My thoughts and writings of lost mines began and concluded with the Blue Bucket Placer deposit. The area of search covers six Oregon counties, where at the most someone found only two nuggets somewhere in or along the banks on an unnamed watercourse, dry wash or seasonal creek. If anyone ever found gold in or around the actual path of the Meek caravan of 1845 instead of miles away in another direction, as claimed, it still has not been determined. If the location was positively identified, something rich would no longer exist in Oregon either as legend or as story. But the legend lives forever and is indestructible.

Leading them on in their mind, keeping time with the roar of thunder influencing their character, temperament and spirit, the passion of John Frémont for exploring has been passed on to later pioneers. The land and animals are both loved and annihilated. They nearly destroyed the true owners and settlers: the Native Americans. They brought all their bad traits, but this experience changed them, and they developed courage and fairness to match their fates. These trailblazers were individualists who stamped their uniqueness on the land, as did the rare and remarkable people who silently heard the rhythms and pursued the path of gold.

The gold hunters were grizzled old eccentrics who lived in remote camps, chasing long lost dreams and shadows of instant wealth. They were transients with no gainful employment, borrowing money from honest citizens for a grubstake, living on the margins of proper society, gambling and drinking in local saloons, patronizing brothels and thus never fully trusted and accepted. Prospectors added bits of color to an otherwise drab life on the frontier. The supplies they bought at local stores brought them a degree of tolerance. As Mark Twain said, "The only difference between a liar and a miner is a miner has a hole in the ground."

Searching today for lost gold, mines or caches today is much easier than in the days of the frontier, when treasure hunters roamed the vast roadless region of the Golden West. The prospector's life was difficult, picking away at a rock ledge or panning for gold in a stream of freezing water for hours at a time, looking over his shoulder for hostile Native Americans and on the ground for rattlesnakes and, hopefully, not the unexpected claim jumper or bushwhacker. Their meager diet consisted of salted meat, stale bread, beans and sometimes rice, washed down with strong coffee and whiskey. The lack of fresh fruits and vegetables could lead to scurvy, and even the clear mountain streams were a hazard. Drinking water seeped from greenish-blue serpentine rock in the Siskiyou Mountains of Southwest Oregon could cause kidney disease and death.

Luckily, current gold seekers live in the era of modern roads and automobiles. As a modern searcher, I would look first on the western slopes of Wagontire Mountain in Lake County for the Blue Bucket nuggets. After that, if no gold trace is found, I would seek a gold nugget like the one found by George Millican in a boulder at a spring on the northern slopes or canyons of Hampton Buttes, under the Columbia River basalt in pre-tertiary rocks and tuff deposits. I am mindful that both Clover and Leaflet Creeks and canyons yielded manganese from a claim staked in 1971 on the western slopes at the 5,000-foot level of the 6,333-foot butte.

The statement of Eliza Simpson, the daughter of L.M. Simpson, is one of the more accurate accounts of the finding of the shining nuggets. Eliza was only five years old at the time and recounted stories she heard over the years. The nugget or nuggets were not from a stream but taken from a mound of earth. Members of the train who never knew their quality or value examined the nuggets. The Meek train then trekked to the Crooked River, where the toolbox containing the nuggets were lost. Gold exists somewhere immediately south of the Crooked River. Other pioneers place the wagon overturning at Maupin on the Deschutes River, highlighting the conflicting accounts of the whole journey. Miss Simpson, later Mrs. L.W. Loughary, repeats the fanciful story of how one of the older girls of the party picked up shinning nuggets and carried them in her apron. On reaching the wagons, she placed them in a blue painted bucket, thus giving rise to the name Lost Blue Bucket Mine.

I would trek to the reaches and banks of Camp Creek, where searchers started in the late 1850s to seek traces of visible gold, like ones found in the chicken droppings by Mrs. Cecil Bennett McKenzie, knowing that finding anything at all is virtually nil. I would even get out of my automobile somewhere in the path of the Meek Party, hike to an unnamed wash and look for a single gold nugget. The discovery occurred in a level area traversed by wagon trains. The search should go no farther west than the upper reaches of Soldier Creek and north of Pringle Flat, where the Tetherow-led train traveled west to Pilot Butte. It was guided there by a Warm Springs native. Bear Creek and the Maury Mountains centering on Drakes Peak is not gold-bearing terrain but is an excellent hunting area for petrified wood and agates.

The Blue Bucket Placer exists, according to the *Harney Times* newspaper, where gold exists in quantities in three gulches of Trout Creek, yielding $50,000 from placer mining beginning in 1891. In addition, Soldier Creek, Rattlesnake, Coffeepot and Cow Creek, ten or more miles southeast of Trout Creek, contain some traces of gold and are much nearer the path crossed by the Meek Caravan than Trout Creek and the Harney Mining District, which lies twenty miles northeast of Burns in the Silvies River watershed.

The Peter Mortimer Canyon northeast of Harney City is the site of gold claims staked by Bill Calterson, Ike Miller, Bob Copeland and Scotty Hayes. The *Oregonian* reports that "the gold is not so plentiful after all. There is some gold there, but it is all in bedrock and there is little or no water to be had for mining."

The country rock is a porphyritic andesite underlying the larger hills in this region. The Meek caravan, according to Tiller and Clark, traveled south from Pine Creek to either East Cow Creek or Big Rock Creek and to the Harney Basin. One or two small gold nuggets eroded from the bedrock of Mortimer Canyon, giving rise to the legend of the Blue Bucket Mine when Dan Herren found a nugget or two in September 1845.

The other main area to look for gold in Oregon is in the Siskiyou Mountains. No major placer deposit discovery occurred after 1904. There is still hope in an area known for gold pockets; a small one or two exist in Southern Oregon, lying undiscovered, although Roy Briggs and his brothers made their find at the Wounded Buck Mine 120 years ago. Still, one can hope and dream of a find. I hope my writing about mines lost and found will make everyone informed and even entertained about Oregon gold legends and continue the search following Frémont's Path during a summer holiday. Maybe someone will find an ore sample or "Strike It

Prospector David Brigg. His son Roy discovered the Wounded Buck Mine. Grants Pass Courier, *1904, 58962*.

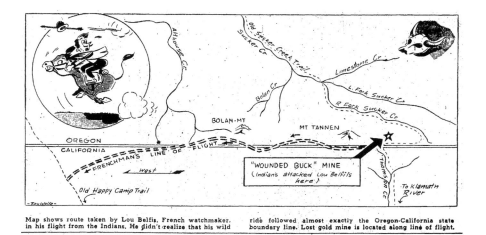

Map shows route taken by Lou Belfils, French watchmaker, in his flight from the Indians. He didn't realize that his wild ride followed almost exactly the Oregon-California state boundary line. Lost gold mine is located along line of flight.

Frenchman Lou Belfils finds and loses the Wounded Buck Mine. Oregonian, *January 18, 1948, page 47.*

Moderately Rich." For me, I would be happy to find a single "Blue Bucket" nugget or small pocket anywhere in Oregon.

The true treasure I found in these stories is doing historical research and writing about them. I learned to write by authoring stories for *Western Treasures* and *Lost Treasure* magazines beginning in 1972, and I continue to do so and maybe hunt for a trace of gold. The only gold I found was a minute amount of color in my pan and flakes of mica, which floated away. The search will go on every time I travel to Central and Eastern Oregon, where I seek to uncover a gold nugget.

GENERAL BIBLIOGRAPHY

Bancroft, Hubert Howe. *History of Oregon*. Vols. 1 and 2. San Francisco, CA: The History Company, Publishers, 1888, 330, 512–16.

Fish, Frank L. *Buried Mines and Lost Mines*. Chino, CA: Amador Publishing Company, 1961.

Gold and Silver in Oregon. Salem: State of Oregon Department of Geology and Mineral Industries, 1968.

Hult, Ruby El. *Lost Mines and Treasures of the Pacific Northwest*. 2nd ed. Portland, OR: Binfords and Mort, 1960, 46–131.

———. *Treasure Hunting Northwest*. Portland, OR: Binfords and Mort, 1971.

Jameson, W.C. *Buried Treasures of the Pacific Northwest*. Little Rock, AR: August House Publishers, 1996.

Latham, John H., ed. *Famous Lost Mines of the West*. Conroe, TX: True Treasure Publications, 1971. Chapters on Blue Bucket, South Umpqua, Frenchmen, Cave of Gold and lost Oregon mines.

MacArthur, Lewis L. *Oregon Geographic Names*. 6th ed. Portland: Oregon Historical Press, 1992.

Oregon Historical Society. Bibliography file and index. Portland, Oregon.

Probert, Robert. *Lost Mines and Buried Treasures of the West*. Berkeley: University of California Press, 1977, Oregon chapter, 385–407.

SPECIFIC BIBLIOGRAPHY

Introduction

Bartlett, John. *Familiar Quotations*. Boston: Little, Brown and Company, 1938.
Brewer, William H. *Up and Down California in 1860–1864*. Berkeley: University of California Press, 1966, 482, 484.
Hood, Thomas. "Gold!" In Bartlett, *Familiar Quotations*, 391.
Rogers, Will. "Last Press Release at Fairbanks, Alaska, August 15, 1935." In Bartlett, *Familiar Quotations*, 859.

Chapter 1

Beebe, Beatrice B. "Hunt for the Blue Bucket Diggings." *Overland Monthly*, August 1929, 252, 255.
Bend (OR) Bulletin. "Carved Inscription on Limb of Juniper Tree Puzzle to Central Oregon Historians." April 27, 1849, 9.
Clark, D.S. "Blue Bucket." *Portland (OR) Daily Bee*, February 6, 1869.
Clark, Keith, and Lowell Tiller. *Terrible Trail: The Meek Cutoff 1845*. Caldwell, ID: Caxton Printers Ltd., 1966, 107–21.
Hancock, Samuel. *The Narrative of Samuel Hancock, 1845–1860*. New York: McBride, 1927.
Herron, W.H. "Letter to the Editor." *Oregonian* (Portland, OR), March 7, 1922.
Gold Annual. "Pieces of Eight Letter." 1974, 68–69.
King, Elsie. "Big Summit Still Has Gold." *Oregon Journal* (Portland, OR), March 7, 1948, Magazine Section, 7.
Latham, F.H. "Oregon's Lost Blue Bucket Mine." *True Treasure* (October 1966): 43–46.
Lockley, Fred. "The McNemee's and Tetherow with the Migration of 1845." *Oregon Historical Quarterly* 25 (December 1924): 353–60.

McNary, Lawrence A. "Route of Meek Cuff-Off, 1845." *Oregon Historical Quarterly* 35 (March 1934): 1–10.

Oregonian. "Another Blue Bucket Story." July 20, 1917. In addition, *Oregon Historical Society Scrapbook* 85: 78.

———. "Blue Bucket in Tygh Valley," letter by Ruth Herren Leonard. April 28, 1919, 8.

———. "The Blue Bucket Mine." Letter to the editor, April 12, 1885, section 3, 1.

———. "Discovery of Blue Bucket Mine Real: Early Oregon Days Recalled by George Millican." April 27, 1919, section 2, 6.

———. "Doctor Bruney's Search." October 24, 1864, 3.

———. "Found Blue Bucket Mine: Death of Dan Herren Recalls Early-Day Stampedes for Gold." July 21, 1908, 10.

———. "Pioneer Days: How Colonel T.R. Cornelius and Party Crossed Plains." July 5, 1885, 1.

———. "Pioneer Woman's Mystery Solved by Grandchildren." October 5, 1950, section 2, 8.

———. "Where Was Blue Bucket?" April 9, 1919, 12.

Parker, Samuel (signed as Blue Buckett). "The Blue Bucket Mines." *Oregonian*, May 6, 1885, section 3, 1.

Pollard, Lancaster. "Blue Bucket Mine Story Tracer to Meek Train." *Oregonian*, February 19, 1956, 47.

———. "Controversy Still Rages over Discovery of Mine." *Oregonian*, January 29, 1956, section 1, 19.

———. "Gold from Famous Blue Bucket Mine First Carelessly Used as Fish Sinkers." *Oregonian*, December 4, 1955, 36.

———. "Scientific Safari Determines Where Blue Bucket Mine Is Not." *Oregonian*, November 24, 1958.

Powers, Alfred. "Mystery of the Blue Bucket Mine." *Oregonian*, July 17, 1949, Magazine Section, 14, 15.

Redman, Arthur H. "Blue Nugget Mine: Not Where Commonly Believed." *Western Treasures* (February 1976): 36–37.

Riggs, Jon L. "Overlooked Bit of History: First Gold on the Pacific Coast Was Found in Oregon." *Oregonian*, November 1, 1903, 28.

Scott, Harvey W. *History of the Oregon Country*. Vol. 3. Cambridge, MA: Riverside Press, 1923, 336–38.

Sunday Oregonian (Portland, OR). "Prospector Ends Search for Blue Bucket Gold." June 10, 1960, 30.

Tetherow, Solomon. Letter to the Editor. *Oregon Spectator* (Oregon City, OR), March 18, 1847, 3.

Chapter 2

Fidler, W.W. "Personal Reminiscences of Samuel L. Simpson." *Oregon Historical Quarterly* 15 (1914): 264–76.

Hillman, John W. "Discovery of Crater Lake." Letter to *Oregonian*, March 10, 1886, 4.

Jones, Randall. "Prospectors Search Long for Legendary Lost Mine." *Sunday Oregonian*, August 29, 1926, section 4, 10.

Oregon Journal. "Samuel L. Simpson." January 8, 1956, Magazine Section, 12.

Simpson, Samuel L. "The Lost Cabin." *Overland Monthly*, November 1872; and *Oregonian*, November 3, 1872, 1. Published posthumously in *Oregon Native Son* (September 1900): 202–8.

Vincent, Dale. "Who Will Find Lost Cabin Mine?" *Oregonian*, April 25, 1948, Magazine Section, 4, 7.

Chapter 3

Anderson, Nancy Dorman. "Oregon's Bohemia Mines." *True West* (November–December 1965): 24–5, 50–51.

Bohemia Nugget (Cottage Grove, OR), December 1899. Oregon Historical Society Manuscript No. 586.

Callaghan, Eugene, and A.F. Buddington. *Metalliferous Mineral Deposits of the Cascade Range in Oregon*. U.S. Department of the Interior. Washington, D.C.: U.S. Government Printing Office, 1938, 82–84.

Dalles (OR) Mountaineer. August 17, 1895, 4.

Lane County Reporter (Eugene, OR). "Another Lost Frenchmen's Mine." November 1959, page 23.

———. "Lost Mine at Johnson Meadows." August 1958.

———. "Old Timer Says: Them Gold Mine Stories Ain't True!" October 1958, 14.

———. "The Story of the Lost Frenchmen's Mine." September 1958, 10.

Oregonian. "Bohemian Mines." July 15, 1951, Magazine Section, 10–11.

———. "Find Lost Mine Too Late." August 16, 1908, 6.

———. "New Strike in Bohemia." January 20, 1899, 5.

———. "Octogenarians to Seek Lost Gold Mine." July 27, 1908, 1.

———. "An Old Story Retold—A Tale of Hidden Treasure in the Cascade Mountains." August 13, 1895, 7.

———. "Rich Ore Found on Laurel Hill." July 11, 1927, 1.

———. "Sandy Claims Staked." July 11, 1927, 1.

———. "Where Did Horsethief Meadow Get Its Name?" August 1, 1917, 39.

Redman, Arthur. "Lost White Cliffs Gold." *Lost Treasure*, February 1976, 31.

———. "The Mt. Horeb Mine." *Lost Treasure* (March 2011): 32, 33.

Salem (OR) Capital Journal. "Minto Pass Misnamed Declares Gates Pioneer, Who First Saw Route." June 18, 1927, 1, 7.

Treasure. "Oregon Curiosities." No. 19 (1939). Works Progress Administration. Washington, D.C.

Vincent, Dale. "Legend of the Lost Rocks Treasure." *Oregonian*, June 27, 1948, Magazine Section, 3.

Chapter 4

Atkinson, Paul. "Oregon's Buried Treasures." *True West* (July–August 1966): 46, 4.

Bancroft, Hubert Howe. *History of Oregon*. Vol. 2. San Francisco, CA: The History Company, 1888, 520, 521.

Henson, Michael. "Buried Chest of Coins." *Lost Treasure* (May 1993): 51.

Killebrew, Gene. "Gold, But Where?" *Oregon Journal*, March 11, 1951, Magazine Section, 3M; April 22, A5; April 30, 1951, 3.

Oregonian. "When Death Struck on the Oregon Trail." September 11, 1938, 85.

Oregon Journal. "Modoc Anne Treasure Sought in East Oregon." April 1, 1959, 1.

———. "Owyhee Gold Cache No Joke, to Indian." April 2, 1959, 12.

———. "Searchers Still Seeking Lost Cave, Gold Mine." April 3, 1959, 2.

Owyhee Avalanche (Homedale, ID). "Idaho State Historical Reference Series: Battle of Three Forks and the Owyhee Cannon." June 5, 1866, 1, 2.

Chapter 5

Applegate, O.C. "Buried Treasure in Klamath County." *Klamath County Echoes*. Klamath County Historical Society, Volume 1, 1964, 38, 39.

Bend (OR) Bulletin. "Crystal Cave Still Waiting to Be Found." November 24, 1973, section 2, 1–3.

Brogen, Phil H. "Crystal Cave in Oregon Found, Lost, Now Hunted." *Oregonian*, November 24, 1946, 21.

Burney, Dr. E.H. "Search for the Meek's Cut Off Mines." Letter to the editor. *Oregonian*, July 20, 1864, 3.

Drago, Harry Sinclair. *Lost Bonanzas: Tales of Lost Mines of the American West*. New York: Dodd, Mead and Company, 1966, 158–66.

Griffin, Dorsey. "Book Review: Western Treasure Trails." *Oregon Historical Quarterly* 100, no. 1 (1999): 86, 87.

The Insiders' Guide to Oregon. "Lost Crystal Cave." Volume 2, Section 10. Christmas Valley, Oregon.

Jenkins, William A. "Lost Oregon Mine." *Treasure World* (October–November 1973): 49.

Jones, Merle. "Lost Crystal Cave." *Gold Annual* (1971): 47, 48.

Leverett, Richard. "The Lost Forest." *Oregonian*, June 24, 1973, F-5.

Ratzlaff, Michael. "Blue Bucket: The Legend Revisited." *Lost Treasure* (October 1988): 20–222.

Shaw, Leslie. "Blue Bucket Mine, Group Believes Fabled Site Found in Lake County." *Lakeview Lake (OR) County Examiner*, April 28, 1960, 1, 4.

———. "Gold Discovery Revives Legend: Paisley Strike May Be Former Blue Bucket." *Lakeview Lake (OR) County Examiner*, March 12, 1925, 2.

———. "The New Blue Bucket Mine Story." *Lakeview Lake (OR) County Examiner*, May 5, 1960.

Wheeler, Dan. "Lost Oregon Loot." *Lost Treasure* (January 1976): 38.

Chapter 6

Ashland Tidings. "Ed Schieffelin's Lonely Death." May 17, 1897.

Giesecke, Eb. "Clues to Buried Treasure." *Oregonian Rotogravure Magazine*, October 14, 1956, 23.

Goza, Lou. "Lost Mine of the South Umpqua." *Treasure Trails of the West* (Winter 1975): 7–12.

Henson, Michael Paul. "Rogue River Cinnabar." *Lost Treasure* (September 1980): 40.

Holbrook, Steward H. "Ex-Oregon Youth Real He-Man of the West." *Oregonian*, Magazine Section, September 4, 1932, 5.

Moore, Richard E. "The Silver King: Ed Schieffelin, Prospector." *Oregon Historical Quarterly* 87 (Winter 1986): 367–87.

Oregon Historical Society Scrapbook. "Yamhill County History," 35, 164.

Oregonian. "Clue to Stagecoach Hold Up Seen in Tree Carving." April 19, 1933, 3.

———. "Frozen Man Rescued." January 16, 1923, 5.

Oregon News-Review (Roseburg, OR). "Missing Red Blanket May Be Clue to Ed Schieffelin's Lost Mine in Canyon Creek Region." April 15, 1948.

Rogue River Courier (Grants Pass, OR). "$2,000 A Day Taken Out on Williams Creek: Harrison Brothers and Others Stake Out Dozen Claims in Past Week." May 22, 1908, 1.

Vincent, Dale. "Lost: Ed's Lost Red Blanket and Rich Gold Mine." *Oregonian*, Magazine Section, March 31, 1946, 8.

———. "Lost Saddle Horn Mine." *Oregonian*, Magazine Section, February 22, 1948, 8.

———. "Oregon Lost Treasure: Six Sacks of Gold Nuggets." *Oregonian*, October 12, 1947, 67.

———. "Thars Gold, They Say in Southern Oregon." *Oregonian*, February 17, 1946, Magazine Section, 2.

White, Victor H. "Some Truth about Gold." *Gold Annual* (Summer 1976): 41, 42.

Chapter 7

Chipman, Art. "Sheepherders Lost Gold Mine." *Treasure World* (July 1969): 47.

Couture, J.A. "Missing Bandit Caches." *Lost Treasure* (December 1976): 28, 29.

Friedman, Ralph. "Hells Canyon Loot." *Lost Treasure* (February 1978): 24, 25, 26.

Gieseck, Eb (aka Giles Beck). "Lost Treasures of Oregon: Bear Creek Mine." Unpublished manuscript. Central Branch Library, Portland, Oregon, 1956, 4.

Gold Annual. "Pieces of Eight." Letter on Blue Bucket Mine. 1974, 68.

Henson, Michael Paul. "Mineral Outcropping." *Lost Treasure* (September 1980): 41.

Hushner, J.L. "Bucket Find Recalled." Letter. *Oregonian*, March 1, 1922, 10.

Jameson, J.C. "Sinkhole Treasure." *Lost Treasure* (March 1995): 20.

Oregonian. "Dave Tucker, Reformed Holdup Man, Became Officer of Bank." November 16, 1960, 29.

———. "Death Ends Gold Hunt." March 18, 1915, 3.

————. "Discovered at Last: The Far-Famed Blue Bucket Mine Located in Harney County." October 20, 1891, 10.

————. "Mysterious Robbery Cleared Up." July 27, 1930, 37.

Simmons, Randy. "$20,000 in Oregon Gold Coins." *Treasure Search* (June 1975): 34–7.

Simmons, R. Neil. "Gold of the Nez Perce." *Lost Treasure* (November 1979): 42, 44.

Snider, Leonard E., Jr. "Lost Golden Ledge." *True Treasure Magazine* (August 1969): 52, 53.

True West. "Oregon's Buried Treasure." August 1966, 25, 46, 47.

ABOUT THE AUTHOR

Arthur (Art) H. Redman was born in Portland, Oregon, and graduated from Portland State University, earning a degree in geography. His father was a rockhound, and the family dug for agates, gems and minerals all over the Pacific Northwest. Art H. became interested in writing after *Lost Treasure* magazine published his first story in 1972. Since then, he has written over sixty articles for *Lost Treasure*, *Eastern and Western Treasure*, *Treasure Cache* and *Oregon Coast* magazines. He has gold-panned, recovering only black mineral-bearing sands and colors and flakes of mica, which floated off. His treasure research has led him to walk the ground of old-time prospectors and treasure seekers who appear in this book.

Visit us at
www.historypress.com